WILD BOUNTY

A Special Edition Game Cookbook

By Jim and Ann Casada

NORTH ★ AMERICAN ★ HUNTING ★ CLUB

MINNETONKA, MINNESOTA

About the Authors

South Carolinians Ann and Jim Casada grew up in households where wild bounty figured prominently in daily fare, and that has continued to be the case in their life together. They are the authors of an earlier work on game cooking, *The Complete Venison Cookbook*, and have been major contributors to several volumes on game cooking. Also, Jim edited *From Campsite to Kitchen: Tastes and Traditions of America's Great Outdoors*, for the Outdoor Writer's Association of America (OWAA). A full-time freelance outdoor writer, Jim currently serves as the president of OWAA. In addition to his joint efforts with Ann on this and other game and fish cookbooks, he has written or edited more than 20 books and contributed to many North American Hunting Club books. Both Jim and Ann are avid outdoor enthusiasts who enjoy living close to nature, savoring the products of the good earth, and sharing that *Wild Bounty* with readers like you.

✦ ✦ ✦ ✦ ✦ ✦ ✦ ✦ ✦

Wild Bounty
A Special Edition Game Cookbook

Printed in 2008.

Tom Carpenter
Creative Director

Heather Koshiol
Book Development Coordinator

Jenya Prosmitsky
Cover Design and Production

Gina Germ, Julie Cisler
Book Production

Becky Landes
Book Design

Phil Aarrestad
Commissioned Photography/Design Coordinator

Ron Essex
Assistant Photographer

Robin Krause
Food Stylist

Susan Hammes, Susan Telleen, Genie Zarling
Assistant Food Stylists

15 16 17 / 11 10 09 08
ISBN 10: 1-58159-163-2
ISBN 13: 978-1-58159-163-7
© 2002 North American Hunting Club

North American Hunting Club
12301 Whitewater Drive
Minnetonka, MN 55343
www.huntingclub.com

TABLE OF CONTENTS

ACKNOWLEDGMENTS

One of the enduring joys of being closely connected to the outdoors is sharing experiences with others of a similar turn of mind. Tales tall and true, campfire chats, reliving hunts past and planning those yet to come, family outings to pick berries or gather nuts, and related activities … all loom large in this process of caring and sharing. Yet to our way of thinking, there is nothing that quite compares with exchanging, sampling and savoring recipes from nature's larder. Whatever the occasion and wherever the place, be it a rustic back country camp or a holiday dining table set with the finest crystal and silver, game and other wild foods are truly special. They become even more so when family and friends are involved.

Such is the case with *Wild Bounty*. We owe debts of gratitude not only to the individuals named below but to all those who have enriched our lives over the years as we partook of dishes and delicacies offered up by the natural world. First and foremost, we must thank those who nurtured us and served as mentors in shaping our ongoing love affair with the wild world. Grandpa Joe Casada kept a shining spark in a wonderstruck lad's eyes with his storytelling of hunts that took place late in the 19th century, and Commodore Casada gave me that most precious of gifts, a love of hunting. Ernest Fox shared his passions for the field with Ann, his only daughter, and both our mothers, Lucy Fox and Anna Lou Casada, knew well how to handle nature's treasure trove in the kitchen.

To those who provided recipes or offered helpful tips, we are deeply appreciative. They include Judy Lyon, George Mayfield, Rick Snipes, Nancy Davidson, Frankie Ledford, Kaye Upgren, Ruth Buckley, Steve and Denise Wagner, Gail Wright, Elaine Tanner and Etah Kirkpatrick. Our daughter and son-in-law, Natasha and Eric Getway, contributed both through encouragement and through their own budding apprenticeship in the wonderful world of game cookery.

Any book involves input and effort by individuals other than the authors, and certainly such is the case with the present work. We owe much to the efforts of Tom Carpenter, Heather Koshiol, Jen Guinea and their colleagues in the Book Department at the North American Hunting Club. Their guidance and encouragement are solid foundations underlying the conception, preparation and ultimate completion of this book.

Finally, we are both appreciative of just how many truly good and gracious people earn their livelihood, as we do, from connections with the outdoors. To these friends and members of the South Carolina Outdoor Press Association, the Southeastern Outdoor Press Association, the Outdoor Writers Association of America, we express our thanks, and the same applies to those in the outdoor industry in general. We bow in gratitude for what they mean to us not merely from the perspective of this book but in our lives.

—*Jim and Ann Casada*

WELCOME ...

... and thanks for joining the North American Hunting Club!

Hunting offers so many rewards. Dreaming of the hunt, gathering gear, scouting, making plans ... getting ready is half the fun. And then you get to go hunting!

Maybe you love bowhunting from your treestand. Or calling in a gobbler through the spring woods. Or hunting deer during the gun season. Or heading west or north or south (or wherever) for bucks, bulls, bears or other big game. Or walking the fields for pheasants and the woods for grouse, maybe with a good dog at your side. Or waiting wide-eyed for a gang of ducks or geese to set their wings and come on in.

But no matter what your hunting passion—and you may have more than one—there's another great reward, and this one comes after the hunt: the wild bounty of game meat you bring home.

That's why we're proud to present you with this special edition *Wild Bounty* game cookbook! Here are over 100 incredible game recipes to help you create some of your greatest game meals ever. From venison, turkey and upland birds to small game, waterfowl, and even a selection of creations from some of nature's other great bounties ... you will love this cookbook and all the ideas it offers.

There's no reason ever to be bored with game meat. It is always lean, healthful, full of flavor ... and it becomes especially delicious when you pair it with the right recipe idea. The next time you need one of those game cooking ideas, you'll know where to turn.

Enjoy your membership in this wonderful, one-of-a-kind hunting club, and enjoy your *Wild Bounty*!

Tom Carpenter
Editor—North American Hunting Club Books

VENISON

Venison figured prominently in human diet long before the first Europeans set foot on American soil, and the meat continued to be a staple food item until late in the 19th century. Incidentally, in the context of venison as a food-stuff, it should be noted at the outset that the word "venison" applies not only to whitetails but to any ungulate or, in Webster's words, "animal of the deer kind." That consideration should be kept in mind when preparing these recipes. In most

cases the recipe will work just as well for elk, mule deer, pronghorn or moose meat as for that of the whitetail; and when ground venison or stew meat is involved, such is virtually always the case. In other words, while most of what follows in this chapter focuses specifically on whitetails, users of the cookbook should not consider this a limiting factor if they happen to be fortunate enough to have other big game in the larder.

While the deer in particular meant vital sustenance for pioneers, along with the occasional

welcome break from everyday drudgery to hunt, there was a great deal of prodigality associated with early hunting of the animal. So much was this the case, in fact, that the combination of market hunting, poor conservation practices, no seasons or limits and related factors led to a dramatic decline in whitetail numbers. Indeed, in the first half of the 20th century precious few Americans, sportsmen or not, knew the joys of eating venison. All of that has changed over the last two generations, thanks to one of the century's great wildlife come-

back sagas. Today whitetail numbers are at record highs, and over much of the nation deer hunting ranks at the top of the list of favored hunting pursuits.

Almost 90 percent of the

Member Ronnie Butler of Allons, Tennessee, with a good Kentucky whitetail.

country's population lives within reasonable driving distance of places where whitetails can be hunted with quite realistic expectations of success. Furthermore, hunting has proven to be a vital management tool, and as deer numbers continue to soar, longer seasons and more liberal limits are the word of the day. Fortunately, venison is as tasty as the animal is abundant, and the size of a deer is such that the hunter who manages to put a deer or two in his freezer each fall has the makings of scores of meals for the coming months.

"Bringing home the bacon" in the form of a nice deer leads to a real sense of accomplishment, and making full and proper use of the meat completes the cycle of ethical sportsmanship that every hunter should practice. Enjoying the benefits of this marvelous game animal ends on the table, but the whole process is exceptionally fulfilling.

LEMON VENISON STEAK

4 slices bacon
1/2 large onion, chopped
1 tablespoon sugar
10 (1-inch-thick) venison steak cutlets from backstrap
Juice of 1 lemon
Lemon pepper

Fry bacon in a cast iron skillet. Remove slices from the pan, leaving 2 tablespoons drippings in skillet and reserving remaining drippings. Add onion to drippings and sprinkle with sugar; cook until onion is tender. Remove onion and return reserved drippings to the skillet. Place cutlets in the skillet; squeeze a small amount of lemon juice on each cutlet and season with lemon pepper. Cook quickly; meat is best if cutlets are still slightly pink in the center. Add crumbled bacon and onion to cutlets and reheat. Serve immediately with wild rice.

SERVES 3 - 4

LOIN STEAKS WITH RASPBERRY SAUCE

1 pound loin steaks
1/3 cup Dale's steak seasoning
1/3 cup water
1/2 stick margarine
1 garlic clove, minced
1/2 cup raspberry jam

Marinate loin in Dale's steak seasoning and water, drain. Melt the margarine and add garlic. Sauté briefly. Add loin and cook to desired doneness. Remove loin and de-glaze pan with jam. Serve as sauce for dipping loin.

NAHC BENEFIT: *NORTH AMERICAN HUNTER* MAGAZINE

Your membership includes a subscription to our information-packed, full-color magazine written for hunters by hunters. This is a publication for NAHC members only. You can't find it on the newsstands, and you must be a current member to receive it.

Shrimp-Stuffed Tenderloin

SHRIMP-STUFFED TENDERLOIN

1 whole venison tenderloin
$1/2$-1 cup Italian salad dressing
12 whole shrimp, cooked and peeled
1 teaspoon Old Bay
1 tablespoon butter, melted
2 teaspoons lemon juice
1-2 slices bacon

Cut loin lengthwise to within $1/4$ - $1/2$ inch of bottom to butterfly. Place loin in Italian dressing to marinate for at least 4 hours. Cook shrimp in water seasoned to taste with Old Bay and peel. Place shrimp end to end inside loin. Melt butter in microwave and add lemon juice; drizzle over shrimp. Close meat around shrimp and secure with toothpicks (or string). Place bacon strips over shrimp and secure with toothpicks. Place loin on a rack in broiler pan and roast at 400°F for about 40 minutes or until rare. (An instant-read meat thermometer is very helpful here.) Meanwhile, prepare Wine Sauce.

WINE SAUCE

$1/2$ cup butter (the real thing)
$1/4$ cup finely chopped onion
$1/2$ cup sliced mushrooms
1-2 large garlic cloves, minced
$1/2$ cup white wine
$1/2$ teaspoon Worcestershire sauce

Melt butter. Sauté onion, mushrooms and garlic until tender. Add wine and Worcestershire sauce and simmer slowly to reduce to about half. To serve, slice loin, remove toothpicks, and spoon on wine sauce.

Tip: Serve with baked brown rice and baked apricots; both can be placed in the oven while the roast cooks. Add a green salad and you have a delicious meal.

TIPS ON CLEANING AND PROCESSING

Two of the most common reasons for inferior or poor-tasting venison are improper cleaning and processing. Whether you live in bitterly cold climates or the sunny South, you should field dress your deer as soon as it is retrieved. Moreover, once the entrails have been removed, a stick or similar means should be employed to keep the body cavity open. This lets the meat cool down more quickly. For gut-shot animals, be sure to clean away every vestige of stomach contents, and no matter where the shot hits, trim away bloody bits and bone fragments.

Processing venison is a fine art and one that is seldom practiced in proper fashion. Understandably, commercial processors are anxious to follow a rapid turn-around approach which means "meat in, meat out." Yet for the finest in taste and tenderness, venison should be aged in a cooler for a week to 10 days at temperatures within a degree or two of 38°F. Ideally, the hide should be left intact during the aging process, although seeking a processor willing to do this often can be an exercise in futility. At the very least, insist on several days of aging.

VENISON TENDERLOIN WITH TOMATO BASIL SAUCE

4 venison loin steaks
3 tablespoons butter or margarine, divided
2 tablespoons olive oil
$1/2$ cup minced vidalia onion
1 garlic clove, minced
$1/2$ cup red wine
1 cup mushrooms, thinly sliced
$1/2$ cup heavy cream (skim milk can be used)
1 medium tomato, peeled and coarsely chopped
4 large fresh basil leaves, chopped
$1/4$ teaspoon salt
$1 1/2$ teaspoons coarsely ground black pepper
 Pat steaks dry. Rub pepper onto both sides of each steak.

In large heavy skillet, melt 2 tablespoons butter and olive oil over high heat. Add steaks and cook until browned and to desired doneness. Transfer steaks to warmed dish and loosely cover with foil to keep warm.

Add remaining 1 tablespoon butter to skillet. Add onion and garlic and sauté for 1 minute. Add wine to skillet and heat to boiling, stirring to scrape up any browned bits. Add mushrooms and cook, stirring frequently until softened, for about 3 minutes. Add cream, tomato and basil and simmer until mixture begins to thicken for about 1 minute. Season with salt and pepper. Spoon sauce over steaks and serve.

SERVES 4

VENISON LOIN MEDALLIONS WITH CHERRY SAUCE

1 cup low-salt chicken stock or broth
1 cup beef broth
1/2 cup cherry liqueur
1/3 cup red ruby cherry pie filling
1 tablespoon cornstarch dissolved in 1/4 cup water
3 tablespoons butter, divided
*8 venison loin steak medallions
    (about 1/2 inch thick)*

Combine chicken stock and beef broth in small, heavy saucepan. Boil until liquid is reduced to 1 cup (about 15 minutes). Add cherry liqueur and boil until liquid is reduced to ¾ cup (about 5 minutes). Whisk in cherry pie filling and simmer until sauce starts to thicken. Add cornstarch dissolved in water and stir until sauce thickens. Whisk in 1 tablespoon of the butter. Season sauce with salt and pepper if desired. Set aside.

Sprinkle venison with salt and pepper. Melt remaining 2 tablespoons of the butter in a large non-stick skillet over medium-high heat. Add venison to skillet and cook to desired doneness. Place 2 medallions on each plate and top with cherry sauce.

SERVES 4

Blueberry Backstrap

BLUEBERRY BACKSTRAP

2 tablespoons butter, melted

4 venison loin steaks, cut ¹/₂ inch thick

   Juice and peel of one large fresh lemon
   (about 2 tablespoons)

1 cup chicken broth

4 tablespoons butter

1 cup fresh blueberries

Several generous dashes ground cinnamon

Several dashes ground ginger

Salt and freshly ground black pepper to taste

Melt 2 tablespoons butter in large skillet and cook venison loin steaks until medium-rare and browned on both sides. Place on platter and keep warm. De-glaze skillet with lemon juice and peel and chicken broth. Cook over high heat to reduce liquid to about ¹/₂ cup. Lower heat to medium and add 4 tablespoons butter, whisking one tablespoon in at a time. Add blueberries, cinnamon, ginger, salt and pepper. Pour blueberry sauce over steaks and serve immediately.

<u>SERVES 4</u>

Tip: Frozen blueberries may be used.

MERLOT LOIN

1 large garlic clove, minced
1 teaspoon freshly ground black pepper
1/2 teaspoon Italian seasoning
2 tablespoons plus 2 teaspoons olive oil
1 venison loin, cut into 1-inch-thick steaks
2 tablespoons butter (the real thing), divided
2 tablespoons chopped onion
1/2 cup sliced mushrooms
1/2 cup beef bouillon
1/4 cup merlot wine
1 teaspoon Worcestershire sauce

Place minced garlic, pepper, Italian seasoning and 2 teaspoons of the olive oil in a bowl and mix well. Rub into loin steaks and refrigerate for 2 - 3 hours.

Pour remaining 2 tablespoons of the olive oil in a skillet and add 1 tablespoon of the butter. Heat to medium high and add steaks. Cook about 4 minutes per side. Do not overcook. Centers of steaks should be pink. Remove steaks from pan and add onion and mushrooms. Sauté briefly and add beef bouillon, merlot wine and Worcestershire sauce. Increase heat to high and reduce liquid by half. Blend in 1 remaining tablespoon of the butter and pour sauce over steaks. Serve immediately.

SERVES 3 - 4

WORCESTERSHIRE STEAKS

3 - 4 venison steaks

MARINADE

1/4 cup Worcestershire sauce
1/4 cup olive oil
2 tablespoons lemon juice
1/2 teaspoon onion salt
1 garlic clove, minced
1/2 teaspoon black pepper

Mix marinade ingredients and place in a sealable plastic bag. Add steaks and marinate for 3 - 4 hours in refrigerator. Grill steaks over hot coals or broil. Do not overcook. About 4 - 5 minutes per side is usually adequate. Serve immediately.

DIJON LOIN STEAKS

BATTER

1/3 cup Dijon mustard
3 tablespoons water
2 teaspoons Worcestershire sauce
1 garlic clove, minced
1/2 teaspoon Italian seasoning

1 cup dry, fine bread crumbs (from whole wheat bread)
1 pound venison loin steaks
2 tablespoons canola oil

Combine all batter ingredients and mix well; place in a shallow dish. Place bread crumbs in second shallow dish. Dip venison loin steaks first in batter to coat, then dredge in bread crumbs. Place canola oil in non-stick skillet and cook steaks over medium-high heat. Cook about 5 minutes or until golden brown on both sides. Do not overcook and turn only once. Steaks should still be pink in the center. Serve immediately.

SERVES 4

ERIC'S SPECIAL STEAK MARINADE

3 - 4 venison steaks

MARINADE

1/4 cup Dale's steak seasoning
1/2 cup water
1 tablespoon Worcestershire sauce
1 tablespoon A-1 Steak Sauce
1/2 tablespoon another steak sauce such as Heinz 57, London Steak Sauce, or Crosse and Blackwell Steak Sauce

Mix ingredients well and marinate venison steaks 3 - 4 hours. Grill to desired doneness and serve immediately. Do not overcook steaks; they should still be pink on the inside.

Tip: The secret is to use different kinds of steak sauces for a blend of flavors.

BOURGUIGNON VENISON

2 medium onions, peeled and sliced
2 tablespoons olive oil
2 pounds venison, cut into 1-inch cubes
1½ tablespoons flour
½ teaspoon marjoram
½ teaspoon thyme
½ teaspoon pepper
1 (10½-ounce) can beef consommé
1 (10½-ounce) can beef broth, double strength
1 cup burgundy (or other hearty red wine)
1 jar sliced mushrooms or ¾ pound fresh mushrooms
Salt to taste (may not need because of salt in
    canned broths)

Sauté onions in olive oil in Dutch oven until translucent; remove onions and set aside. Add venison to Dutch oven and cook, adding a bit more olive oil if necessary. When browned well on all sides, sprinkle flour, marjoram, thyme and pepper over venison. Stir for about 1 minute to coat venison well and cook flour. Then add consommé, broth and burgundy and stir. Simmer very slowly for about 3 - 3½ hours until venison is tender. Allow to cook down for intense flavor. More consommé and wine may be added if needed. After cooking, return onions to Dutch oven and add mushrooms. Stir well and simmer another hour. The sauce should be thick and dark brown. Serve with a wild and white rice mixture, roasted asparagus, garlic bread sticks and burgundy.

SERVES 8 - 10

GRILLED LOIN STEAKS

1 venison loin

MARINADE

1 cup low-sodium soy sauce
1 large garlic clove, minced
1 tablespoon honey
1 tablespoon steak sauce (your choice)
Several dashes Tabasco sauce

Cut loin into 1-inch-thick steaks. Place in a resealable plastic bag. Mix marinade ingredients well and pour into the bag over steaks. Marinate in refrigerator 3 - 4 hours. Place on grill or use grilling pan and cook on medium high to desired doneness. Do not overcook.

Tip: Do not have the heat too high or the marinade will burn on the exterior of the steaks. The touch of honey adds a great deal to the flavor but does tend to burn if the heat is high. Baked apricots make a wonderful accompaniment to these steaks. Try them with duck or quail also.

BAKED APRICOTS

1 (16-ounce) can apricot halves, drained
15 Ritz crackers, crushed
2 tablespoons light brown sugar
2 tablespoons butter, melted

Place drained apricots in a casserole dish. Roll crackers into crumbs. Sprinkle crackers on top of apricots. Sprinkle brown sugar over crackers. Pour melted butter over top. Bake at 350°F about 15 - 20 minutes or until hot, bubbly and golden brown.

SERVES 2

Tip: If you wish to make a larger casserole, alternate layers of apricots, crumbs and brown sugar.

Grilled Loin Steaks with Marinade

Venison

Loin Steaks with Apricot Mustard Sauce

LOIN STEAKS WITH APRICOT MUSTARD SAUCE

4-6 venison loin steaks
Salt
Black pepper
Butter

Heat a non-stick skillet over medium-high heat; sprinkle the skillet lightly with salt and add steak. Cook until browned and turn steak (sprinkling the pan with salt again before placing back in pan). Cook until steak reaches desired doneness (do not overcook) and sprinkle with freshly ground black pepper. Top steak with a small pat of butter and allow to melt into steak before removing from the pan.

APRICOT MUSTARD SAUCE

½ cup grainy brown mustard
⅓ cup apricot jam
¼ cup brandy

While steaks are cooking, heat mustard, jam and brandy in a small saucepan over medium heat, stirring frequently, until jam has melted and ingredients are well combined. Drizzle sauce over steaks and serve immediately.

<u>Serves 4</u>

PEPPER STEAK

1/2 cup soy sauce
1 teaspoon sugar
1 garlic clove, minced
1 pound venison steak, cut into strips
2 tablespoons olive oil
1 large green pepper, cut into thin strips
1 red onion, thinly sliced
1 cup sliced fresh mushrooms
1/2 cup water
2 tablespoons cornstarch

Combine soy sauce, sugar and garlic. Add venison steak strips. Toss lightly and refrigerate for 3 - 4 hours. Drain steak. In a heavy skillet or wok, add olive oil and heat to medium high; add venison steak strips and stir fry for 3 - 4 minutes; add pepper, onion and mushrooms and stir fry for 3 - 4 additional minutes or until vegetables are tender crisp. Combine water and cornstarch and add to meat and vegetables, stirring constantly until thickened. Serve over rice, pasta or mashed potatoes.

STEAK AND POTATOES

1 pound venison cubed steak
2 tablespoons olive oil
1 (10¾-ounce) can cream of celery soup
1/2 cup milk
1/2 cup sour cream
1/4 teaspoon freshly ground black pepper
16 ounces frozen hash browns, thawed (cubed style)
1/2 cup shredded cheddar cheese, divided
1 (3-ounce) can french fried onions, divided

Brown venison steaks in olive oil in a skillet and set aside. Combine soup, milk, sour cream and pepper. Stir in thawed potatoes, 1/3 cup cheese, and 1/2 can onions. Spoon mixture into 9 x 13-inch baking dish. Arrange steaks over potatoes. Bake, covered, at 350°F for 45 - 50 minutes. Top with remaining cheese and onions and bake, uncovered, for 5 - 10 minutes longer.

THOUGHTS ON COOKING VENISON

Along with problems in cleaning and processing, improper cooking is the other prime culprit in turning off folks who eat venison. Quite simply, too much cooking can ruin many cuts of venison. The finest cuts—backstrap and tenderloin—should still be pink in the middle when taken from the grill, skillet or oven, and much the same is true of cubed steaks, ground venison and roasts. Indeed, the only time venison should be cooked for long periods of time is when it is used in soups, stews or similar dishes.

Using marinades, a meat hammer and good processing will make venison tender and tasty. Overcooking, on the other hand, will mean dry, relatively tasteless meat.

LOIN STEAKS WITH ONION RELISH

1 pound venison loin steaks, cut ¾-inch thick
¼-1 teaspoon coarsely ground black pepper
2 tablespoons olive oil
1 tablespoon butter or margarine
1 tablespoon lemon juice
1 large vidalia onion, thinly sliced and separated
  into rings
½ cup zinfandel wine
½ teaspoon dried basil, crushed
¼ teaspoon salt

Rub both sides of steaks with ground pepper. In large non-stick skillet, heat olive oil and butter over medium-high heat; add steaks, drizzle with lemon juice and cook for about 4 minutes on each side for medium doneness. Remove the steaks and reserve drippings. Keep steaks warm.

Cook onion in drippings over medium heat for 5 - 7 minutes or until tender crisp. Add wine, basil and salt. Cook until most of the liquid has evaporated. Arrange steaks on plates and spoon onion relish on top.

<u>SERVES 4</u>

Tip: Leftovers make good sandwiches. Try them topped with mozzarella cheese. Broil to heat and melt cheese.

CRAB STUFFED VENISON STEAK ROLLS

STUFFING

1/4-1/2 stick butter or margarine
1 garlic clove, minced
1/4 cup chopped celery
1/4 cup chopped onion
1/2 pound imitation crab, cut into small chunks
    (or the real thing)
1 tablespoon dried parsley
1/2 teaspoon dried cilantro
Salt and pepper to taste

Melt butter; add garlic, celery and onion; sauté vegetables until soft. Add crab meat, herbs, salt and pepper. Remove from pan.

STEAKS AND WINE SAUCE

2 tablespoons butter or margarine
1 garlic clove, minced
4 venison cubed steaks (flatten if necessary)
4 large slices onion
1 cup zinfandel wine
1/2 cup sour cream
Salt and pepper

Add butter to pan and lightly cook garlic; add steaks and quickly brown on both sides. Remove from pan and let cool enough to handle. Place stuffing in the center of steaks and roll. Secure with as many toothpicks as needed. Cut 4 large slices of onion and place in the pan. Place steak rolls on top of each onion slice. Pour wine over steaks. Cover and simmer for 15 - 20 minutes or until tender. Carefully remove onion and steak rolls from pan and place on a dish. Add sour cream to pan drippings and cook, stirring constantly until warm but not boiling. Salt and pepper to taste. Pour over steaks and serve immediately.

MUSTARD FRIED VENISON STEAKS

1 pound venison cubed steaks
1/2 cup prepared mustard
2/3 cup flour
1 teaspoon salt
6 tablespoons canola oil

Brush venison cubed steaks on both sides with prepared mustard. Mix flour and salt and dredge mustard-painted steaks in flour. Heat canola oil in a skillet and quickly cook floured steaks until golden brown. Serve immediately.

Tip: Any kind of mustard works well—try yellow, brown, Dijon or whatever you like best. An inexpensive paint brush makes "painting" the steaks quick and easy.

GREEK VENISON WRAP

3 slices bacon
1 small vidalia onion, thinly sliced
4-5 medium mushrooms, thinly sliced
1/2 teaspoon sugar
1 venison loin, thinly sliced
Lemon pepper (to taste)
1 teaspoon lemon juice
2 tortilla wraps, warmed
2 tablespoons sour cream
Fresh spinach leaves
3-4 tablespoons feta cheese, crumbled

Fry bacon in a skillet until brown; remove from pan, crumble and set aside. Add onion and mushrooms to pan and sauté until onions are translucent. Add sugar and stir well. Add venison and sprinkle generously with lemon pepper. Add lemon juice and sauté until venison is cooked (but still pink). Warm tortillas in microwave with a damp paper towel on top. Place sour cream in the center of tortilla, add several leaves of spinach, feta cheese, crumbled bacon and venison mixture. Wrap and serve immediately.

SERVES 2

BASIL VENISON

1 pound cubed venison steaks, cut into thin strips
Italian salad dressing

Slice and/or chop mixed fresh vegetables of your choice: onion, yellow squash, zucchini, carrots, sugar snap peas (if frozen, defrost). Place strips of steak in nonmetal container and cover with Italian salad dressing. Marinate for at least 30 minutes (3 - 4 hours is better).

BASIL BUTTER

2 ounces fresh basil (2 bunches)
10 ounces butter or margarine
1 large garlic clove, minced
1/8 teaspoon black pepper
4 tablespoons grated Parmesan cheese

Remove large stems from basil and wash. Shake off excess water and dry. Place basil in a food processor. Add other ingredients and pulse until basil is chopped and all the ingredients are mixed well. Store in refrigerator and use as needed. Keeps for 7 days.

Cook vegetables in basil butter until partially done. Drain venison and add to vegetables. Continue cooking until venison is done. Serve immediately over rice.

Tip: Also try this basil butter with pasta and shrimp; it is delicious.

CHILI STEAK AND SALSA

1 teaspoon chili powder
1-2 garlic cloves, finely minced
1/2 teaspoon salt
1/2 teaspoon black pepper
3/4-1 pound cubed venison steaks
1 tablespoon olive oil
1/4-1/2 cup prepared salsa

Combine chili powder, garlic, salt and pepper. Rub evenly into both sides of steaks. Place olive oil in non-stick skillet over medium heat until hot. Add steaks and cook to desired doneness (for about 8 minutes). Turn steaks to brown evenly. Serve immediately with prepared salsa placed on top of each steak.

Tip: For a special treat, prepare a fresh tomato salsa.

BOURBON MUSTARD STEAK

1 pound cubed venison steaks
Salt and pepper to taste
2 tablespoons Dijon mustard
2 tablespoons butter or margarine
2 tablespoons olive oil
2 green onions, chopped
2 tablespoons bourbon
1 can mushrooms, drained
1/4 teaspoon dried chives
1/4 teaspoon dried parsley
1/4 teaspoon dried Italian seasoning
4 tablespoons sour cream

Season steaks with salt and pepper and spread mustard generously on both sides of steaks. Melt butter in skillet and add olive oil. Brown steaks quickly on medium-high heat until desired doneness is reached. Do not overcook. Remove steaks. Add green onions and sauté. Add bourbon and cook until most of the liquid evaporates. Add mushrooms, herbs and sour cream, blending thoroughly with pan juices. Pour over steaks and serve immediately with rice.

CHIVE STEAKS

1 pound cubed venison steaks

CHIVE BUTTER

1/4 cup butter or margarine, at room temperature
2-3 tablespoons fresh chives, chopped
2 teaspoons freshly squeezed lemon juice
1/2 teaspoon salt
1/4 teaspoon pepper

In a small bowl, combine butter, chives, lemon juice, salt and pepper. Using a fork, mix vigorously until blended. Place about half the butter mixture in a sauté pan over medium-high heat. Add steaks and cook quickly to desired doneness. Just before removing from pan, place a bit of the butter mixture on each steak and allow to melt before removing steaks. Serve immediately.

Serves 4

Tip: Try broiled tomatoes with steaks.

Cubed Steak Italiano

CUBED STEAK ITALIANO

2 tablespoons olive oil

1 pound cubed venison steaks, cut into strips

1 onion, sliced

1 green pepper, cut into strips

1 garlic clove, minced

1 cup sliced mushrooms

1 (26-ounce) jar meatless spaghetti sauce

1 teaspoon dried basil

Salt and pepper to taste

In a large skillet, heat olive oil and sauté steak strips, onion, green pepper, garlic and mushrooms until done. Stir in spaghetti sauce, basil, salt and pepper. Cover and simmer for 15 - 30 minutes to blend flavors. Serve over pasta of your choice.

<u>SERVES 4</u>

Crockpot Roast with Cranberries

CROCKPOT ROAST WITH CRANBERRIES

1 (10½-ounce) can double-strength beef broth
½ can water
¼ teaspoon ground cinnamon
2-3 teaspoons cream-style prepared horseradish
1 (16-ounce) can whole berry cranberry sauce
1 venison roast (3-4 pounds)
Salt and pepper to taste

Place broth, water, cinnamon, horseradish and cranberry sauce in medium saucepan; heat to boiling while stirring constantly. Place venison roast in crockpot. Pour sauce over roast and cook on low for 6 - 8 hours or until roast is tender. Pass juice with roast.

SERVES 8

Tip: Leftovers are good cold, sliced for sandwiches.

JERKY

1½ pounds venison, partially frozen

MARINADE

¼ cup Worcestershire sauce
¼ cup soy sauce
1 teaspoon liquid smoke
1 teaspoon onion powder
½ teaspoon garlic powder
¼ teaspoon black pepper
Several dashes hot sauce (Tabasco)

Partially freeze venison and slice into ¼-inch pieces. Mix marinade ingredients and add venison slices; marinate for 16 - 24 hours in refrigerator. Cover bottom rack of oven with foil. Place strips of venison on top rack. Set oven temperature on 150°F and crack door slightly. By cracking the door, temperature will be between 130 and 140°F (at 150°F the jerky tends to be too crunchy). Dry jerky for 6 - 8 hours. Store in airtight containers.

Tip: Partially freezing the venison makes slicing thinly much easier.

PARTY PÂTÉ

2 pounds venison, cooked
1 medium onion, chopped
1 garlic clove, minced
1 hard-cooked egg
½ cup Hellman's mayonnaise
1 stick butter, softened (do not substitute)
¼ cup bourbon (high quality)
½ teaspoon salt, or to taste
¼ teaspoon pepper, freshly ground, or to taste
Bayleaf

Place venison, onion, garlic and egg in food processor and pulse until smooth. Add mayonnaise and softened butter and mix only enough to thoroughly blend. Add bourbon, salt and pepper and blend well. Mold into a ball and top with a bay leaf. Wrap securely with plastic wrap and refrigerate overnight. Remove bay leaf, garnish with chives and serve with Melba toast, party rye, or assorted crackers.

HAMBURGER STEAK WITH ONION TOPPING

2 tablespoons canola oil
1-1½ cups sliced sweet onions
1-2 tablespoons water
¼ teaspoon paprika
Black pepper to taste
1 pound ground venison
Salt to taste

Heat canola oil in large skillet and sauté onions until tender. Add water while sautéing onions if needed to prevent sticking. Stir paprika and black pepper into onions; remove onions from pan and keep warm. Season ground venison with salt and shape into 2 large 1-inch-thick patties. Put hamburger steaks in onion-flavored oil and cook over medium heat until browned on both sides and desired doneness is reached. Arrange steaks on 2 plates and top with reserved, cooked onions.

QUICK VENISON MAC

½ pound ground venison
1 small leek (or onion), chopped
1 garlic clove, minced
1 tablespoon olive oil
1 (14-ounce) can diced tomatoes
1 (8-ounce) can tomato sauce
1 cup water
¼ teaspoon chili powder
⅛ teaspoon cumin
¼ teaspoon sugar
¼ teaspoon black pepper
1 cup uncooked elbow macaroni
3 tablespoons fresh oregano, chopped

In a skillet, brown venison, chopped leek and garlic in olive oil. Be sure to crumble venison as it cooks. Add tomatoes, tomato sauce and water and bring to a boil. Add all other ingredients except fresh oregano and return to a boil. Reduce heat, cover and simmer for 15 minutes or until macaroni is tender. Add oregano and serve immediately.

CHOPPED STEAK AND GRAVY

2 teaspoons dry beef onion soup mix
1 pound ground venison
1 teaspoon Worcestershire sauce
Salt and pepper to taste
2 tablespoons olive oil
2 tablespoons flour

Microwave onion soup mix in ¼ cup water until onions are tender and add to ground venison with Worcestershire sauce, salt and pepper. Handle gently and form into patties. Place olive oil in a non-stick pan. Add patties and cook until done (6 - 8 minutes). Remove from pan. Add flour and make a roux. Stir constantly for 1 minute. Add 1 cup water (or more if needed) and stir until smooth and thick. Add patties and simmer for 10 - 15 minutes. Serve with rice.

VENISON EGGPLANT PARMIGIANA

1 large eggplant, or 3-4 small eggplants
Salt to taste
1 pound ground venison
½ cup chopped onion
2 garlic cloves, minced
1 tablespoon olive oil
1 (16-ounce) can diced tomatoes
1 (8-ounce) can tomato sauce
3 tablespoons fresh basil, chopped
½ teaspoon black pepper
1 tablespoon cherry preserves
1 egg, beaten
½ cup cracker crumbs (saltines)
1-2 tablespoons olive oil
2 cups shredded mozzarella cheese

Peel and slice eggplant, place on paper towels and sprinkle with salt; cover with more paper towels. Let set while preparing sauce.

In large skillet sauté venison, onion and garlic in 1 tablespoon of the olive oil until meat is no longer red. Add tomatoes, tomato sauce, basil, salt and pepper and cherry preserves. Stir well and simmer for 15 - 20 minutes.

Rinse eggplant and pat dry. Dip in egg and then cracker crumbs and quickly brown in remaining 1 - 2 tablespoons of the olive oil. Spray baking dish. Layer eggplant, 1 cup of the cheese, sauce and remaining 1 cup of the cheese. Bake at 350°F uncovered for 15 - 20 minutes or until bubbly and hot.

Deep Dish Potato and Venison Pie

DEEP DISH POTATO AND VENISON PIE

Pastry for double-crust pie (homemade or
 purchased)
1 cup grated, peeled potatoes
1/4 cup chopped celery
1/2 cup grated carrots
1/4 cup chopped leeks
2 teaspoons Worcestershire sauce
1 teaspoon A-1 Steak Sauce
1 teaspoon dried Italian seasoning
1/4 teaspoon freshly ground black pepper
Salt to taste
1 pound uncooked ground venison

Place bottom crust in 9-inch deep dish pie plate.
Mix all other ingredients and place in pie crust.
Place top crust on pie and seal edges.
Cut vents in top pastry. Bake at 375°F for 15
minutes. Reduce heat to 350°F degrees and bake
for 55 - 60 minutes. This pie is hearty; however, it
is dry and needs to be served with a sauce. We
like this mushroom sauce.

MUSHROOM SAUCE

2 tablespoons butter or margarine
1/4 cup sliced leeks
2 cups sliced fresh mushrooms (wild or button)
2 tablespoons flour
1 cup half-and-half
Salt and pepper to taste

Melt butter and sauté leeks and mushrooms until
tender. Sprinkle with flour and cook for about 1
minute. Add half-and-half and seasonings.
Continue cooking until sauce has thickened. Stir
constantly. Serve over pie slices.

*Tip: This sauce can also be used over steaks, chops or
wild rice with upland game.*

ITALIAN BURGERS

1 egg
1/4 cup oats, regular or quick cooking (do not use instant)
2 tablespoons ketchup
3/4 teaspoon dried Italian seasoning
1 garlic clove, finely minced
2 tablespoons finely chopped onion
1/4 teaspoon salt
1 pound ground venison
4 mozzarella cheese slices
4 hamburger buns or rolls

Lightly beat egg with a fork and stir in oats. Add ketchup, Italian seasoning, garlic, onion, salt and ground venison. Mix well and shape into 4 patties. Broil or grill patties about 12 minutes or until desired doneness is reached, turning once. Top with cheese and broil until cheese melts. Serve on toasted buns with ketchup, lettuce and tomatoes.

FETA BURGERS

1 cup plain yogurt
1/4 cup feta cheese
1/4-1/2 teaspoon ground cumin
1 pound ground venison
1/4 cup finely diced onion
1/2 teaspoon dried cilantro, or to taste
Several dashes of ground ginger, or to taste
Salt to taste
Lettuce
Cucumbers, thinly sliced
Pita bread

Blend yogurt, feta cheese and cumin with a fork until the cheese is finely crumbled. Cover and refrigerate for 1 hour. Combine ground venison, onion, cilantro, ginger and salt to taste. Shape into 4 patties and grill, broil or pan fry until done. Place lettuce and cucumbers in pita bread, add burger and top with 2 tablespoons yogurt sauce.

SERVES 4

BLUE CHEESE BURGERS

1 pound ground venison
1/4 cup finely chopped onion
1/4 cup crumbled blue cheese
1 teaspoon Worcestershire sauce
1/4 teaspoon salt
1/8 teaspoon freshly ground black pepper

Mix all ingredients thoroughly but gently and shape into 4 patties. Grill over hot coals (for about 4 minutes per side) or until burgers have reached desired doneness. Serve on grilled hamburger buns with lots of crisp lettuce, tomato slices and mayonnaise.

SERVES 4

Tip: These can be broiled or cooked in a grilling pan. If grilling, oil the grill top to prevent sticking.

BURGERS WITH BUILT-IN CONDIMENTS

1 pound ground venison
2 tablespoons ketchup
1 tablespoon A-1 Steak Sauce
2 teaspoons mustard
1/2 teaspoon Worcestershire sauce
Several dashes freshly ground black pepper

Thoroughly mix all condiments into ground venison. Form into patties, being careful to form well because condiments make burgers softer. Grill to desired doneness and serve on onion rolls with lettuce, tomato, onion and pickles.

Mexican Burgers

MEXICAN BURGERS

1 pound ground venison
1/4 cup finely chopped onion
1/2-1 teaspoon chili powder (or to taste)
1/4 teaspoon ground cumin
1/2 teaspoon finely minced jalapeño pepper
    (or to taste)
1/2 teaspoon salt
1/4 teaspoon black pepper

Combine all ingredients well and shape into 4 patties. Grill, broil or pan fry to desired doneness. Serve burgers on tortillas (cut burgers in half for a better fit), pita bread, English muffins or hamburger buns with traditional taco toppings of your choice. The toppings might include salsa, shredded cheese, guacamole or chopped avocado, sour cream, lettuce and diced green onions. Serve with Corona and lime wedges or Mexican beer.

Venison

WILD TURKEY

The American wild turkey holds a proud and prominent place in our nation's culinary history. At an early age, schoolchildren learn of the manner in which wild turkeys graced the Pilgrims' tables at the first Thanksgiving celebration, and stories of how America's big game bird offered fine fare on frontier tables fill fictional and factual chronicles of pioneer life. Wild turkeys were incredibly abundant during the early years of European settlement, and surprisingly, given the quarry's modern-day wariness, hunters experienced little trouble in killing them for personal use and the market.

In time, an increasing human presence, roost shooting, the absence of hunting seasons or a conservation ethic, and general prodigality, changed all this. Turkeys disappeared from much of their original range, and by the dawn of the 20th century they had become so scarce as to be a gourmet delight denied all but a select few.

But even then, those privileged to live in regions where there were still wild turkeys—and possessed of sufficient savvy and skill to hunt them successfully—recognized the bird's grand attributes when it came to fine dining. For example, the enduring stories of a grand old Southern sporting scribe, Archibald Rutledge, are laced with descriptions of holiday feasts featuring a wild turkey as the centerpiece. Similar circumstances existed in the home of another South Carolinian, Henry Edwards Davis, author of *The American Wild Turkey* (which many authorities consider the single finest book ever written on turkey hunting). Davis' daughter, Virginia Carroll, tenders a delightful anecdote of her youthful experiences in dining on wild turkey. "I never tasted domestic

Life Member Julian Zielinski of Pinconning, Michigan, with a nice jake.

turkey," she recalls, "until I went off to college. When it was served there, I found the dry breast meat a poor excuse for the juicy, flavorful white meat of wild turkeys I was accustomed to eating."

Those familiar with the savory, succulent flavor of the wild turkey will readily identify with Mrs. Carroll's memories. Today their ranks are much larger than was the case a eneration or two ago, thanks to the still-unfolding saga of the wild turkey's comeback. The story, which must rank as one of this century's most significant wildlife restoration successes, has resulted in the big birds once more roaming remote woodlots and farmlands in great numbers. Wildlife biologists across the country have linked hands with the National Wild Turkey Federation to restore turkeys to their original range and far beyond. Today it is possible to hunt wild turkeys in every state but Alaska. This means that the avid outdoorsman, whether he hunts spring gobblers (which is now the standard approach to the sport) or pursues the rich traditions of fall hunting, has realistic expectations of enjoying a sumptuous feast once or twice a year.

The wild turkey certainly deserves special treatment, for it is a special treat. The recipes that follow, along with interspersed tips on preparation covering subjects such as making use of the complete bird and how to handle your prize in the field, should enable you to prepare and present the wild turkey with all the graciousness and grandeur this noble game bird merits.

DEEP-FRIED TURKEY

1. Clean turkey well (as you do for roasting).

2. Thaw turkey completely and pat dry with paper towels.

3. Do not stuff turkey when deep frying.

4. Rub with dry seasonings of your choice. Suggestions are: seasoned salt and pepper, paprika, cayenne pepper, garlic salt, onion salt, Cajun seasonings or Italian seasonings.

5. Turkey may be injected with liquid seasonings (there are syringes available for this purpose). Some possibilities are: hot pepper sauce, Italian salad dressing or liquid Cajun seasonings.

6. Peanut oil is best for deep frying.

7. You need a very large pot (for example, use a 26-quart aluminum pot for a 16-pound turkey). An outdoor cooker is best for this process.

8. To determine how much oil to use, first fill pot with water and place turkey into water. Water should cover turkey without spilling over. Adjust water level as needed. Remove turkey and note water level (or measure water). Dry pot and turkey well before adding oil. It usually takes 3 to 5 gallons of oil.

9. Heat oil to 300 - 350°F (or until nearly smoking).

10. Very carefully and slowly submerge turkey into hot oil.

11. Cook 3½ - 4½ minutes per pound or until meat thermometer registers 180°F. The turkey tends to float when done.

12. A wire coat hanger hooked to the drumsticks is handy for lowering and raising turkey (or use cotton string draped over outside of pot).

13. Be very careful during the lowering and raising of the turkey.

14. Drain turkey well on paper towels.

15. Wrap drained turkey in foil to keep warm.

16. Allow turkey to rest for 15 - 20 minutes before carving.

17. Carve and enjoy this Southern treat.

ROASTED WILD TURKEY

1 medium onion, cut into chunks
2 ribs celery (with leaves), cut into chunks
2 carrots, cut into chunks
1 bay leaf
1-2 tablespoons margarine or olive oil

Place dressed and cleaned wild turkey in enamel roasting pan. Stuff with onion, celery, carrots and bay leaf. Season turkey with salt and black pepper and rub with margarine. Cover, place in oven and cook at 350°F until done. Baste turkey every 20 - 30 minutes.

There are lots of theories and timetables regarding cooking time; however, investing in an instant read meat thermometer takes a lot of worry out of those special holiday meals. Insert a thermometer into the thickest part of the inner thigh, not touching bone. Temperature should reach 180°F. If you prefer a timetable, use the following guidelines:

- up to 6 pounds, 20 - 25 minutes per pound

- 6 to 16 pounds, 15 - 20 minutes per pound

- over 16 pounds, 13 - 15 minutes per pound

- if bird is stuffed, add about 5 minutes per pound

Stuffing: There is a great deal of dispute over the safety of stuffing fowl. The cavities of wild birds do contain bacteria; to be safe, cook dressing separately in a casserole.

Tips: Some people may say that this method is steaming rather than roasting; however, we feel the breast is not as dry and the cooking time is less. The end result of delicious, moist, golden turkey convinced us that this easy method was our favorite.

If you have leftovers, try some of the following recipes for a change of pace: turkey pie, ring of turkey, que-sadillas, enchiladas or salads. Your family will never know you are serving leftovers.

BASIL PASTA AND TURKEY

4 tablespoons olive oil
1 tablespoon butter or margarine
½ cup chopped onion
½ cup sliced fresh mushrooms
½ cup slivered almonds
2 large garlic cloves, minced
1 pound wild turkey breast, pounded and cut
    into chunks
½ cup sun-dried tomatoes (soaked in hot water)
8 ounces pasta (spaghetti), cooked
2-3 tablespoons fresh basil, chopped
1 teaspoon Italian seasoning
½ cup freshly grated Parmesan cheese

Place olive oil and butter in a large frying pan. Sauté onion, mushrooms, almonds, garlic and turkey breast chunks. Cook until turkey is no longer pink. Add tomatoes, cooked pasta, basil, Italian seasoning and Parmesan cheese. Stir to mix well. Serve immediately and top with additional freshly grated Parmesan cheese.

SERVES 3

WILD TURKEY TENDERS

1 egg
1 tablespoon water
1 pound wild turkey breast, cut into 1-inch strips
1 cup all-purpose flour
½ cup canola oil
Salt and black pepper to taste

Beat egg with water. Dredge turkey strips in flour, dip in egg mixture, then again in flour. Fry in canola oil in cast iron skillet until brown and tender. Season with salt and black pepper. Serve immediately.

SERVES 3 - 4

Tip: If turkey is not tender, cover and steam a few minutes after you have browned the strips. The turkey will not be as crisp but the steaming will tenderize if you have a tough bird.

BLACK WALNUT CRUSTED TURKEY

1 pound wild turkey breast cutlets, pounded with a
    meat mallet
½ cup oil-and-vinegar salad dressing
⅓ cup finely chopped black walnuts
½ cup fresh bread crumbs
1 tablespoon finely chopped fresh chives
1 tablespoon margarine
2 tablespoons olive oil

Place pounded wild turkey breast cutlets in a quart plastic bag. Pour salad dressing over turkey and marinate in the refrigerator for at least 6 hours (or overnight).

Place black walnuts and bread crumbs in blender and process until fine. Add chives.

In large skillet, melt margarine and add olive oil over medium high heat. Drain cutlets and dip into combined black walnuts and bread crumbs; press to coat.

Place turkey cutlets in skillet and reduce heat to medium; cook for 4 to 6 minutes per side until golden brown and the interior is no longer pink. Serve immediately.

SERVES 4

TURKEY TENDERS PARMESAN

1 egg, beaten
½ bottle prepared ranch dressing
1½-2 cups bread crumbs
¼-½ cup Parmesan cheese
8-10 strips wild turkey breast
2 tablespoons olive oil

Combine egg with ranch dressing. Mix bread crumbs and Parmesan cheese. Dip turkey strips in dressing/egg mixture. Then dredge in breadcrumb mixture. Heat olive oil in non-stick fry pan. Be sure olive oil is hot before adding strips. Brown turkey on both sides and cook until turkey runs clear. If turkey is not tender enough, cover pan and simmer a few minutes.

SERVES 2

Black Walnut Crusted Turkey

BASIL TURKEY QUESADILLAS

PESTO MAYONNAISE

1 large garlic clove, minced
1/2 cup slivered almonds and/or pine nuts
1 tablespoon butter or margarine
1/2 cup packed fresh basil leaves
1/3 cup Hellman's light mayonnaise

Sauté garlic and nuts in butter until golden. Place basil, mayonnaise, garlic and nuts in blender. Process until smooth.

4 flour tortillas
Cooking spray
1 cup chopped wild turkey
1 cup shredded cheese (Mexican blend is nice)

Spray bottom of 2 tortillas with cooking spray. Spread pesto mayonnaise evenly over those 2 tortillas. Top with chopped turkey and shredded cheese. Place remaining 2 tortillas on top of turkey and cheese and spray with cooking spray. Place in non-stick frying pan, covered, and cook until brown. Turn and brown until cheese melts and quesadilla is heated. Serve with thinly sliced red and yellow tomatoes and shredded lettuce on top. Garnish with a dollop of sour cream.

SERVES 2

TURKEY FRUIT SALAD

1 (20-ounce) can pineapple chunks
1 red apple, cored, chopped
3 cups cooked rice
2 cups cubed, cooked, smoked wild turkey
1 cup seedless grapes
1/2 cup sliced celery
1 (8-ounce) carton light peach yogurt
2 tablespoons orange marmalade
1 tablespoon grated orange peel
Lettuce leaves

Combine pineapple, apple, rice, turkey, grapes and celery in a large bowl. Combine yogurt, marmalade and orange peel in a separate bowl, mixing well. Add yogurt mixture to fruit and turkey, tossing to mix. Spoon salad into a bowl lined with lettuce leaves.

SERVES 8

TURKEY FLORENTINE PIZZA

1 pound wild turkey breast
3-4 garlic cloves
2 tablespoons olive oil
1 teaspoon dried Italian seasoning
1 cup (or less) ricotta cheese
1/2 cup shredded mozzarella cheese
1 (16-ounce) pre-baked pizza crust
1 (10-ounce) package frozen spinach, thawed, squeezed dry and patted with paper towels
3 tablespoons chopped sun-dried tomatoes marinated in olive oil, drained
1/4 cup grated Parmesan cheese

Preheat oven to 425°F. Rinse turkey with cold water and pat dry with paper towels. Pound with a meat mallet. Cut into 1-inch pieces. In large skillet, heat garlic and olive oil. Add turkey and cook for 10 minutes or until done. Stir in seasoning and remove from heat. Combine ricotta and mozzarella; spread on pre-baked pizza crust. Spread spinach over cheese mixture; add turkey and tomatoes. Sprinkle with Parmesan cheese. Bake pizza at 425°F for 12 - 15 minutes or until crust is golden brown and cheese is melted.

SERVES 4

TURKEY PIE

6 tablespoons butter or margarine, melted
6 tablespoons all-purpose flour
1/4-1/2 teaspoon freshly ground pepper
2 cups homemade turkey broth (or purchased chicken broth)
2/3 cup half-and-half or cream
2 cups cooked wild turkey, chopped
Prepared pastry for 2-crust pie (purchased or homemade)

Add flour and seasonings to butter. Cook for 1 minute, stirring constantly. Add broth and half-and-half and cook slowly until thickened. Add turkey and pour into pastry-lined pan. Top with rest of pastry and pinch edges together. Bake at 400°F for 30 - 45 minutes or until pastry is browned.

SERVES 6

Tip: Try this simple pie using other game (quail, rabbit, squirrel, duck or venison). This is a delicious way to use leftovers. Add vegetables to make turkey pot pie.

WILD TURKEY MEATBALLS

For a very different and tasty appetizer, try these meatballs:

1½ cup ground wild turkey
1 cup finely crumbled cornbread
¼ cup finely chopped, toasted hazelnuts
1 large rib celery, finely chopped
2 tablespoons finely chopped onion (and cooked in a microwave a bit)
¼-½ teaspoon Italian seasoning
¼ teaspoon salt
1 teaspoon dry mustard
½ cup chicken broth
1 egg, beaten

Place all ingredients except broth and egg in a mixing bowl. Add broth and egg, being careful to mix very well. Preheat oven to 375°F while you form meatballs. Shape into 1-inch balls and place on 15 x 10 x 1-inch baking pan which has been sprayed with cooking spray to prevent sticking. Bake at 375°F for 20 - 25 minutes or until meatballs are browned and no longer pink in the center. Meanwhile, place sauce ingredients in large skillet.

SAUCE

1 (16-ounce) can whole berry cranberry sauce
1 tablespoon brown sugar
1 teaspoon Worcestershire sauce
1 tablespoon prepared Dijon mustard with horseradish

Bring to a boil over medium heat. Reduce heat to low and simmer for 5 - 10 minutes stirring occasionally. Add meatballs and heat for 5 - 10 more minutes stirring occasionally. (Meatballs will be heated through and sauce will adhere to meatballs). Serve as an appetizer in chafing dish or slow cooker.

Tip: Cut turkey into chunks and grind in a food processor. Good kitchen shears (we use Gerber's game shears) make chopping the turkey a much easier task. Also, the food processor is ideal for chopping the cornbread, nuts, celery and onion; however, process them separately from turkey because it takes longer to chop turkey than other ingredients. Toasting hazelnuts enhances flavor.

UPLAND BIRDS

Upland bird hunting is one of America's most cherished sporting traditions. The image of a pointer etched against an evening sky—holding staunchly on a sundown covey—is an enduring one, and some of our finest outdoor writing has been produced by individuals for whom bird hunting was the ultimate sporting experience. Men such as Robert Ruark, Havilah Babcock, Nash Buckingham, Archibald Rutledge and Burton Spiller come immediately to mind in this context, and it is well worth noting that these writers sang not only the literary but also culinary glo-

ries of partridges and pheasants, woodcock and grouse.

One measure of a fine sporting scribe is his ability to make you hungry when describing food, and when the featured fare is upland game, those skills seem to reach their apex. Anyone who has read Ruark's *The Old Man and the Boy*, arguably the finest single book ever written on our great outdoors, will have fond memories of the manner in which he described the dining delights furnished by that five-ounce bundle of feathered dynamite he called "the noble quail." Similarly, Nash Buckingham could positively wax poetic on the

glories of a platter of quail flanked by "cathead" biscuits, while Archibald Rutledge's descriptions of plantation game feasts at holidays invariably included mention of upland game birds.

For all that they have been heralded in literature, however, feathered upland game too often receives short shrift in cookbooks. That is both unfortunate and unfair, for when properly prepared there is nothing more delectable or delightful. My paternal grandfather was of the fixed opinion that "there's nothing finer than properly cooked pottiges" (a generic term he used to describe bobwhite quail), and far be it from me to argue with his

thoughts when it comes to game dishes.

No matter where you live, in all likelihood one or more species of upland gamebird is available nearby in relative abundance. Properly prepared,

Life Member Harvey Hull of Detroit, Michigan, with some South Dakota bounty.

all upland game birds are delectable, and the recipes which follow offer a wide variety of approaches to enjoying this hunter's delight.

Upland Birds

QUAIL WITH CURRANT SAUCE

1/2 stick butter

4 quail, cut into serving pieces

1/2 cup currant jelly

Salt to taste

1 tablespoon brandy - or to taste

Melt butter in a heavy skillet. Brown quail slowly. Remove quail. Add currant jelly and stir well while jelly melts. Season with salt to taste. Return birds to pan and baste with sauce. Cover and simmer until quail are tender. Stir brandy into sauce until just heated and serve immediately.

SERVES 2 - 3

Tip: The butter will burn if too hot. If needed, more butter may be added to the sauce. Don't use margarine; the butter does make a difference in this recipe.

HOW TO GET IN TOUCH

Calling our toll-free number or writing to the right department can save a lot of time and confusion when you need to contact us.

By Mail:

Member Services Department

NORTH AMERICAN HUNTING CLUB

P.O. Box 3401, Minnetonka, MN 55343

By Phone:

1-800-922-4868

Member Services Representatives are available Monday through Friday, 7:30 AM to 6:00 PM CST to answer your questions about membership / subscriptions and to process orders.

By E-mail:

memberservices@huntingclub.com

Web site:

www.huntingclub.com

GRILLED QUAIL SALAD

4 quail, cut in half lengthwise through breast

1 cup Italian salad dressing

Marinate quail in Italian dressing (we like Paul Newman's Olive Oil and Vinegar) several hours. Drain well and grill over glowing coals until skin is browned and desired doneness is reached. Alternatively, a grilling pan may be used. Arrange quail on top of Mixed Green Salad and serve with Garlic Vinaigrette Dressing.

MIXED GREEN SALAD

Mesclun mix, Boston lettuce, or your preferred salad mixture

Grated carrots

White mushrooms

Red bell pepper

Cherry tomatoes

Cucumbers

Red onion slices

GARLIC VINAIGRETTE

1 garlic clove, minced

1 teaspoon Dijon mustard

1 tablespoon rice vinegar

1/4 cup heavy cream

4 tablespoons extra virgin olive oil

Several dashes of salt, to taste

Freshly ground black pepper

Place garlic, mustard, vinegar and cream in a small bowl. Slowly add oil while beating with a wire whisk until emulsified; season with salt and pepper.

Arrange lettuce on 4 large plates. Add other salad ingredients arranged in an appealing manner. Top each salad with a quail half and drizzle with garlic vinaigrette. Serve remaining vinaigrette on the side.

SERVES 4 FOR A LIGHT MAIN COURSE.

APPLE QUAIL

1/4 cup flour
1/2 teaspoon salt, or to taste
1/8 teaspoon paprika
6 quail, breasts and legs
2 tablespoons butter
1/4 cup chopped sweet onion
1 tablespoon chopped fresh parsley
1/4 teaspoon dried thyme (or 1/2 teaspoon
    fresh thyme)
1 cup apple juice

Mix flour, salt and paprika; lightly flour quail pieces. Melt butter in heavy frying pan and brown quail. Push quail to one side of pan. Add onion and sauté until tender (add 1 tablespoon more butter if needed to sauté onion). Add parsley, thyme and apple juice. Stir to mix well and spoon juice over quail while bringing all to a boil. Reduce heat, cover and simmer until quail are tender (about 1 hour). Serve quail on a bed of rice with sautéed apples on the side.

Tip: To sauté apples: Melt 3 tablespoons butter in a skillet, add 2 cooking apples (cored and cut into wedges), and sprinkle with 2 tablespoons sugar (more or less depending on how sweet the apples are). Cook, turning often, until apples are lightly browned. Garnish apples with a light sprinkling of cinnamon sugar.

Pheasant in Mushroom Cream Sauce

OREGANO PHEASANT

2 pheasants, cut into serving pieces
All-purpose flour
1/4-1/2 cup butter or margarine
1 (10¾ ounce) can cream of mushroom soup
    with roasted garlic and herbs, undiluted
1 (10¾-ounce) can cream of chicken soup,
    undiluted
1 (4-ounce) can sliced mushrooms, rinsed
    and drained
1/4 teaspoon dried oregano
1/2 teaspoon minced garlic
1/4 cup sour cream
1/2 cup white wine
Salt and pepper to taste

Dredge pheasant in flour. Meanwhile, melt butter in 9 x 13-inch baking dish in 325°F oven. Place pheasant in dish, cover and bake at 325°F for 1 hour. Combine soups, mushrooms, oregano, garlic, sour cream, wine, salt and pepper. Turn pheasant pieces and pour sauce over pheasant. Bake, uncovered, for 1 hour or until tender.

SERVES 4

PHEASANT IN MUSHROOM CREAM SAUCE

1 pheasant (1½-2 pounds)
1/2 cup onion
1 cup fresh sliced mushrooms
2 tablespoons butter or margarine
3 ounces cream cheese
1 (10¾-ounce) can cream of mushroom soup
1/4 cup water
2 tablespoons milk
1/2 cup shredded carrots
1 tablespoon parsley flakes
1 teaspoon instant chicken bouillon

Salt and pepper pheasant and place in greased baking dish, skin side down. Bake at 350°F for 30 minutes.

Meanwhile, prepare mushroom cream sauce: Sauté onion and mushrooms in butter until tender. Add remaining ingredients and stir until smooth.

After pheasant has baked for 30 minutes, turn pheasant and add mushroom cream sauce. Cover and continue baking until tender. Serve with wild rice.

KAYE'S PHEASANT WITH WILD RICE CASSEROLE

1/2 pound fresh mushrooms, sliced, or 4-ounce can
    mushrooms
2-4 tablespoons butter
1 onion, finely chopped
1 cup finely chopped fresh parsley
1/2 cup chopped celery
1 (10¾-ounce) can cream of mushroom soup
1/2 soup can milk
1 cup grated cheddar cheese
2 cups cooked wild rice
2 pheasants, cut into pieces
Flour
Paprika

Cook mushrooms in butter for 5 minutes. Remove mushrooms; add onions, parsley and celery to pan; cook until onions are tender and golden. In separate saucepan, heat soup and milk. Add cheese. Add to wild rice and mushroom mixture. Roll pheasant in flour and brown in shortening. Pour rice mixture into greased casserole. Top with pheasant. Sprinkle with paprika. Cover and bake at 325°F for 1 hour.

Tip: Top with slivered almonds if you wish.

DOVE BREAST APPETIZERS

Dove breasts
Italian salad dressing
Bacon slices, cut in half and precooked a bit in the
    microwave

Marinate dove breasts in your favorite Italian dressing (we like Paul Newman's Olive Oil and Vinegar) for at least 4 hours. Wrap bacon strip around each dove breast and secure each with toothpick. Place on hot grill and cook for approximately 8 - 10 minutes, turning often or until center is pink.

Tip: Optional stuffings for variation: wrap each dove breast around a jalapeño pepper half and onion slice, or water chestnut, or pepper cheese before putting bacon around dove breasts.

GAME BIRD TIDBITS

Typically, the heart, liver and gizzard of upland game birds are discarded during the cleaning process. But for those willing to put in a bit of extra effort, these tidbits offer the potential for some real taste treats. For example, dove or quail hearts saved over the course of an entire season of hunting, then marinated and grilled, are delightful hors d'oeuvres.

Similarly, hearts, livers and gizzards can be cooked, mixed with some boiled egg and onion, run through a blender and then salted and peppered to taste. The result is a nice pâté which can be spread on crackers or toast points and served with pre-dinner drinks.

RICK'S CREOLE DOVES

16-20 dove fillets
1/2-1 stick butter or margarine
Chef Paul Prudhomme's Creole Seasoning

Quickly sauté dove fillets in butter and sprinkle with Creole seasoning as you cook the doves. Do not overcook. Doves are best if still pink inside. Serve immediately.

Tip: These are a delicious appetizer. You'll find you cannot cook them fast enough for your guests!

ROASTED GROUSE

1 large onion, chopped
1 rib celery, chopped
1 carrot, chopped
1 garlic clove, minced
1 tablespoon olive oil
1 grouse, cleaned and dressed
1/2 teaspoon salt
1/2 teaspoon pepper
1/2 teaspoon paprika
1 teaspoon flour
1 tablespoon margarine

Sauté onion, celery, carrot and garlic in olive oil until wilted. Stuff grouse with vegetable mixture. Place in roasting pan. Sprinkle with salt, pepper, paprika and flour. Dot with margarine. Bake at 400°F for 15 minutes. Reduce heat to 350°F and cook about 40 minutes longer or until tender.

GROUSE IN CREAM SAUCE

2 grouse
Salt and pepper to taste
1 onion, quartered
1/2 cup diced celery (with leaves)
1/4 cup diced carrots
1 bay leaf
1 cup water

Place grouse in Dutch oven and add remaining ingredients. Simmer 1 1/2 - 2 hours or until tender. Remove birds and cool. Break meat into small pieces and stir into cream sauce.

CREAM SAUCE

1 cup fresh sliced mushrooms
2 tablespoons butter or margarine
1 (10 3/4-ounce) can cream of chicken soup
1/2 cup milk (add more or less to get as thick or
    thin as you prefer)
Salt and pepper to taste

Sauté mushrooms in butter. Add soup and milk and heat. Stir until smooth. Add grouse pieces and adjust seasonings. Serve over toast, homemade biscuits, or in pastry shells.

Tip: Mushroom soup is an alternative choice. This is a good way to use leftovers also. Try using turkey, quail, pheasant or rabbit.

UPLAND GAME

Most sportsmen of my generation cut their sporting teeth on upland game, with the occasional quest for feathered game interspersing more frequent daytime hunting for squirrels and rabbits. Nightfall meant the haunting music of a baying pack of hounds singing their hallelujah chorus while hot on the trail of a 'coon or 'possum. For those with a bent for sharpshooting, long-distance shots at whistle pigs (groundhogs) offered some welcome variety and did farmers a real favor.

Squirrel hunting in particular afforded a real primer in woodsmanship, thanks to the emphasis it placed on skills such as stealth in stalking, keen eyesight and optimum use of the sense of hearing, the ability to read sign, and accurate marksmanship. Interestingly enough, there is nothing more uniquely American in the world of sport than bushytail hunting. The treetop tricksters formed a central item of diet on frontier fare, thanks in part to the fact that squirrels were incredibly abundant during the days when the American chestnut reigned supreme in millions of acres of

hardwood forests. Youngsters cut their shooting teeth on squirrels, with a premium being placed on "barking" them in order to retrieve the lead bullet for recasting. Skills thereby honed to a razor's edge played a key role in turning the tide in the American Revolution, most notably at the Battle of Kings Mountain, and until quite recently squirrel hunting remained the single most popular shooting sport over much of the country.

Two great conservation comeback stories, those associated with the white-tailed deer and wild turkeys, have changed matters dramatically in the modern era. The attention of today's hunter focuses in large measure on deer and other big game along with America's "big game bird," and as a result, small game gets relatively little attention. Yet the varied

NAHC editor and Member Tom Carpenter with Max and a Wisconsin cottontail.

approaches to hunting afforded by upland game

retain their historical appeal, and anyone who has sampled and savored the fine fare it can offer knows just how delightful it can be on the table.

The recipes that follow focus primarily on rabbits and squirrels, both of which remain plentiful over much of the country. Indeed, in many states wildlife biologists indicate that the most underutilized game animal is the squirrel. Seasons for upland game typically begin before and continue long after those for deer have come and gone, which means added opportunity to enjoy those precious hours afield which all of us cherish. You will also find some other suggestions for non-traditional game dishes involving 'coons, 'possums and even muskrats; and in that regard, be sure to look at the sidebar on "The Trapper and the Table."

One final thought on upland game seems in order before getting down to the vital matter of fine eating. The future of sport lies with youngsters, and there is no finer way to introduce a budding hunter to the joys of the wild world than through small game hunting. Typically, rabbits and squirrels are plentiful, which means a promise of the action so important in catching and maintaining the interest of those with short attention spans. The targets will be challenging and plentiful, and there's every chance you will come home with a game bag that's not empty. So you have a golden opportunity to teach the ethical values of cleaning and eating what you kill.

ANNA LOU'S SQUIRREL

1-2 squirrels, dressed
Water to cover squirrel
1 teaspoon baking soda
1-2 tablespoons butter

Place dressed squirrel in large saucepan. Cover with cold water, add soda and heat to boiling. Remove from heat and rinse squirrel well under running water (rubbing to remove soda). Return to pan and cover with fresh water. Bring to a boil, reduce heat and simmer until tender. Place squirrel in baking dish, dot with butter, and bake at 350°F until browned and crusty.

Tip: Use the broth from cooking the squirrel to make delicious gravy. Rabbit can be prepared in this manner also. A pressure cooker is good to use for tenderizing a squirrel or rabbit and works well with this recipe.

HASH BROWN POTATOES WITH SQUIRREL

1½-2 cups chopped, cooked squirrel
3 medium potatoes (about 1¼ pound)
⅓ cup bacon drippings or oil
¼-½ cup finely diced onion
½ teaspoon salt
Several dashes freshly ground black pepper

Remove squirrel from bones and chop into small pieces. Peel and coarsely grate potatoes. Put drippings in skillet and heat. Slide potatoes into heated drippings. Sprinkle onion, squirrel, and seasonings over potatoes. Cover and cook moderately fast until potatoes are browned on underside. Stir to blend, turn over, cover and brown on other side. Total cooking time is approximately 10 minutes. Serve immediately.

<u>SERVES 4</u>

Tip: Use kitchen scissors to make chopping the squirrel an easy task. Rabbit or other game can be used. This is a good way to use a few leftovers.

Lemon Wine Rabbit

LEMON WINE RABBIT

1 rabbit

1 lemon, cut in half

Salt and pepper to taste

2 tablespoons butter, melted

1/2 cup chardonnay wine

1 tablespoon chopped chives

1 tablespoon chopped parsley

Skin and clean rabbit. Rub rabbit with lemon halves and squeeze lemon juice on rabbit. Rub with salt and pepper. Cut rabbit into serving pieces. Brush rabbit with melted butter. Place in roasting pan and bake at 400°F for about 10 minutes. Add wine; reduce heat to 350°F and continue cooking until tender for at least 1 hour until tender. Baste occasionally. Top with herbs. Serve with drippings poured over rabbit. Wine drippings may be thickened with flour and water paste if desired.

Squirrel with Lima Beans

SQUIRREL WITH LIMA BEANS

1/4 pound bacon
2 squirrels, dressed and cut into pieces
2 cups dried lima beans, soaked overnight
Flour, salt and pepper
1 onion, chopped
2 ribs celery, chopped
2 carrots, chopped
1 tablespoon sugar
1 cup okra
3 potatoes, diced
2 cups frozen corn
2 (16-ounce) cans stewed tomatoes
1 bay leaf
Dash of thyme and parsley
1/2-1 teaspoon crushed red pepper (as desired)

Dredge squirrel pieces in flour mixture. In Dutch oven, fry bacon and remove. Brown squirrels in bacon drippings; cover squirrels, bacon, beans, onion, celery and carrots with boiling water. Simmer for 2 hours. Squirrel meat may be removed from bones at this point if you desire. Add remaining ingredients and simmer for 1 hour longer or until squirrel and vegetables are tender. If desired, thicken with flour and water paste and adjust seasonings.

SERVES 6 - 8

SQUIRREL AND BISCUIT-STYLE DUMPLINGS

2 squirrels
2 bay leaves
1 cup chopped onion
1 cup chopped celery
3-4 carrots, chopped
Salt and pepper to taste
2 cups water

Cut 2 squirrels into serving pieces. Place in a Dutch oven and cover with water. Add bay leaves and simmer for 1 1/2 hours or until squirrels are tender. Skim if necessary. Squirrel may be removed from the bones at this point and returned to stew if you desire. Add onion, celery, carrots, seasonings and water. Cook for 15 - 20 minutes or until vegetables are tender. Increase heat. Heat stew to boiling.

DUMPLINGS

1/2 cup milk
1 cup flour
2 teaspoons baking powder
1/2 teaspoon salt

Slowly add milk to dry ingredients. Drop by teaspoons into boiling liquid. Cook for 15 - 20 minutes longer or until dumplings are done in the center.

SERVES 4

BACON SQUIRREL OR RABBIT

Strained bacon drippings
2 squirrels (or rabbits), quartered
1/2 cup flour
1/2 teaspoon garlic salt
1/4 teaspoon freshly ground black pepper
1/4 teaspoon paprika
1 1/2-2 cups fine dry bread crumbs
1/2 teaspoon basil (optional)

Cook bacon and strain drippings. Pat squirrel dry with a paper towel. Roll squirrel in flour mixed with garlic salt, pepper and paprika. Dip in and completely moisten with bacon drippings. Dredge in bread crumbs seasoned with basil. Place squirrel in baking dish and bake at 375°F for 30 - 45 minutes on one side; turn and bake on other side for 30 - 45 minutes more or until well browned and tender.

SERVES 4

Tip: Since bacon varies so much in the amount of fat, we did not give an amount; however, be sure to have enough drippings to completely moisten each piece so that the bacon flavor is imparted to the meat. The crumbled bacon would be delicious sprinkled on a spinach salad to compliment the Bacon Squirrel or Rabbit.

NAHC BENEFIT: MANY SPECIAL SAVINGS

Your NAHC membership can save you money in many ways. In addition to saving money on hunting products you can buy through NAHC, you can also take advantage of special member-to-member discounts from other members who guide hunts, own lodges, manufacture equipment or are otherwise involved with hunting. Be sure to check North American Hunter and its Keeping Track section for these special offers.

SQUIRREL (OR RABBIT) BOG

2 squirrels (or 1 rabbit), cut up
Salt to taste
1 medium onion, chopped
2-3 ribs celery, chopped
Pepper to taste
1/2-3/4 pound smoked venison sausage (or kielbasa)
1 cup uncooked long-grain rice

Sprinkle squirrel pieces with salt and place in Dutch oven with enough cold water to cover completely. Add onion, celery and pepper. Bring to a boil; reduce heat, cover and simmer until squirrel is tender and readily separates from the bones. Remove squirrel, saving broth. Let squirrel cool, remove meat from bones.

Measure broth back into pot. (It is not necessary to drain onion and celery.) Add water if necessary to make four cups liquid. Return squirrel to pot. Cut smoked sausage into 1/4-inch slices. Add to pot along with rice; stir. Add more salt and pepper to taste. Bring to a boil, reduce heat, cover and simmer for about 30 minutes or until most of broth is absorbed into rice or until rice grains are fluffy and tender.

SERVES 4 - 6

Tip: This traditional dish from the South Carolina Low Country is versatile, and various types of meat (such as chicken, venison, wild turkey or other game birds) can be used.

SMOTHERED RABBIT

1 rabbit, quartered
Flour
3 tablespoons butter or oil
1 onion, sliced
Salt and paprika
1 cup sour cream

Sauté flour-coated rabbit in butter until it is browned. Cover rabbit with onion slices and sprinkle with salt and paprika. Pour sour cream over rabbit. Cover and simmer for 1 hour or until the rabbit is tender. Serve with rice.

Squirrel (or Rabbit) Bog

Upland Game

WATERFOWL

In days of yesteryear, there was a time when waterfowl figured prominently on the menus of the finest restaurants in major American cities along the Eastern seaboard and the Mississippi flyway. This was long before passage of the Lacey Act or, for that matter, state or federal game laws. In Chesapeake Bay and in the bayous of Louisiana, in the wetlands of the Carolina coast and in the marshes of the American heartland, skilled market hunters, some of them equipped with punt guns, killed waterfowl in the untold tens of thousands. Even as late as the World War I era, hunters were regularly taking daily bags of ducks numbering in the dozens. "

Inevitably market hunting, poaching and mindless waste took their toll, and by the time the first federal waterfowl stamp was issued in the mid-1930s, the outlook for ducks was dismal indeed. Thanks to decades of unrelenting efforts, the ducks (or at least most species of them) have begun to come back, while some species of geese have become so numerous as to pose major threats of destruction of nesting ground habitat. Today the waterfowl picture, while not exactly rosy, is brighter than it has been in a long time.

That means that once more hunters can sit shivering in a blind, listening to the whistling wings of dawn while waiting for the magic moment of legal shooting time to arrive, with a real sense of expectation. Limits have become a bit more liberal and seasons somewhat longer, and today's waterfowler does not have to worry about wearing out the hulls of his shotshells from loading and unloading them.

Instead, chances of coming home with a brace or two of ducks, or maybe even filled limits, are quite good. That means that once again, after the passage of all too many decades, hunters can enjoy not only the wonders of a dawn sky wearing a mantle of pink filled with gabbling ducks; they can also relish the wonderful dishes offered by properly prepared waterfowl.

Life Member William F. Wedding Jr. of Madisonville, Kentucky, with some dabblers.

Orange-Glazed Duck

ORANGE-GLAZED DUCK

1 wild duck
1 teaspoon salt
1/2 teaspoon pepper
1/2 teaspoon paprika
1/4 teaspoon ginger
2 cups orange juice
1 teaspoon lemon juice
1 tablespoon currant jelly

Rub cleaned duck with mixture of salt, pepper, paprika and ginger. Place in roasting pan (on a rack) and bake at 400°F for 1 hour. Drain off fat. Pour mixture of orange juice, lemon juice and currant jelly over duck. Baste frequently and continue to bake until tender.

ROAST STUFFED DUCK

1 wild duck, dressed and cleaned
2 tablespoons butter, softened
Salt
Freshly ground black pepper
1 (16-ounce) can sauerkraut
1½ cups water

Rub duck inside and outside with butter and generously sprinkle with salt and pepper. Stuff with sauerkraut. Tie securely with wings and legs close to body. Sear in a roasting pan, breast side up, in 400°F oven for 15 minutes. Add 1½ cups water and baste. Reduce oven temperature to 300°F and cook 30 minutes per pound. Baste often. Add more water if needed.

Tips: People who do not like sauerkraut really like this. A blow torch is a quick and easy way to remove down after dry picking duck.

WRIGHT DUCK WITH STUFFING

1 wild duck
1 teaspoon salt
1 teaspoon oregano
1 teaspoon paprika
½ teaspoon black pepper
¼ cup olive oil
¼ cup lemon juice

Place duck on a rack in roasting pan. Mix above-listed ingredients and pour evenly over duck. Bake covered for 1½ hours at 350°F. Bake uncovered for 30 minutes at 350°F.

STUFFING

1 (14½-ounce) can chicken broth
1 package Knorr vegetable soup mix
3 ribs celery, chopped
1 medium onion, chopped
¾ stick butter or margarine
4 cups herb-seasoned stuffing (any brand)

Place broth and soup mix in saucepan. Heat to boiling and let simmer for 5 minutes. Sauté celery and onion in butter. Mix stuffing with broth mixture and add celery and onion. Serve as a side dish with duck.

SERVES 4

Tip: Wild rice and baked apples go great with this dish.

BARBECUED WRIGHT DUCK

SAUCE

1 cup ketchup
½ cup lemon juice
¼ cup brown sugar
1 tablespoon Worcestershire sauce
½ teaspoon salt
½ teaspoon pepper
½ teaspoon paprika
1 teaspoon hot sauce
2 wild ducks, halved

Mix sauce ingredients in saucepan. Heat to a low boil and simmer for about 5 minutes. Place duck halves on a rack in roasting pan. Spread with barbecue sauce and cover with foil. Bake covered at 325°F for 1½ hours. Remove foil and spoon on remaining sauce. Bake uncovered for 20 more minutes at 375°F.

SERVES 4 - 6

BUCKLEY DUCK

2-4 ducks
Bacon drippings
Salt and pepper
Several garlic cloves, minced
Parsley
Flour
Beef bouillon
Mushroom soup (optional)

Brown ducks quickly in a heavy cast iron skillet using bacon drippings. Remove ducks and cool slightly. If you will use the same skillet for baking in the oven, wipe all fat from skillet. (Duck fat is sometimes strong.) Make a small slit in each side of the duck breasts. Insert into this slit a mixture of salt, pepper, chopped garlic (a lot) and parsley. Then place the ducks in cast iron skillet or Dutch oven with lid. Make gravy using browned flour and beef bouillon and pour over ducks. Cover and bake in oven at 350°F until ducks become tender (approximately 1½ hours). Check ducks periodically for tenderness; sometimes one duck can be removed and another left to cook longer. When ducks are done, remove meat from bones by slicing on either side of breast bone and peeling it away. Put meat back in gravy and serve with rice and Mayhaw jelly. A can of mushroom soup may be added to gravy if you desire.

SERVES 4 - 6

To skin or pluck?

The never-ending debate over whether to skin or pluck ducks and geese really has some simple answers. Make your decision on the basis of how much time you are willing to spend in the cleaning process, how you intend to cook the waterfowl, and what you want in the way of self-basting fat for the cooking process.

When it comes to roasting or baking, the cooking process will definitely benefit from the skin being present. It provides some fat that in effect self-bastes the waterfowl as they cook, and the skin also serves to retain moisture and prevent the dryness which can be the bane of wild game cooking.

For grilling, use in stews or gumbos and the like, skinned waterfowl work quite nicely. As for the time factor, skinning certainly expedites the cleaning process, although if you are fortunate enough to have access to one of the machines which remove feathers, plucking may not be necessary.

In the final analysis, the matter is one of personal preference, and waterfowl with or without their skin can be quite tasty.

BAKED DUCK BREASTS

2 duck breasts, filleted into 4 pieces
1 1/2 sticks butter (no substitute)
4 bay leaves
1 tablespoon poultry seasoning
1 tablespoon dried chives (or 3 tablespoons fresh)
1 tablespoon parsley flakes
1/2 teaspoon garlic salt
Black pepper to taste
Dash cinnamon

Fillet the breasts out of 2 ducks and wash thoroughly. Line a baking dish or pan with aluminum foil; leave enough foil to seal when the ingredients are added. Cut butter into chunks and distribute evenly over ducks. Place a bay leaf on each fillet. Sprinkle remaining ingredients on top of the duck breasts. Close foil securely and bake for 1 hour 15 minutes or until tender. Remove bay leaves before serving. Serve with orange sauce.

ORANGE SAUCE

1 cup orange juice
1/4 cup sugar
1 teaspoon nutmeg
1 tablespoon cornstarch

In a medium saucepan, combine orange juice, sugar and nutmeg. Bring to a rolling boil, add cornstarch and stir constantly until thickened. Remove from heat.

Serves 4

Tip: This quick and easy orange sauce is great with duck, goose, turkey, game birds or venison.

Duck Stroganoff

DUCK STROGANOFF

3 tablespoons canola oil
8 duck breasts, filleted and sliced thinly
1 medium onion, finely chopped
3 tablespoons butter
1 pound fresh sliced mushrooms
6 tablespoons flour
2 cups half-and-half or cream
1/2-1 teaspoon salt
1/4 teaspoon black pepper
1/8 teaspoon nutmeg
2 tablespoons white wine
1 cup sour cream

Heat canola oil in a large skillet over medium heat. Add duck and onion and cook quickly. Duck should still be pink inside. Remove. Add butter and mushrooms and sauté until mushrooms are tender. Remove mushrooms and add flour to pan drippings. Stir constantly for about 1 minute. Add half-and-half, salt, pepper and nutmeg. Stir constantly until thickened. Add duck, onion and mushrooms and simmer briefly to heat through. Add wine and sour cream to hot mixture and heat but do not boil. Serve immediately over wild rice.

SHERRIED DUCK

2 tablespoons olive oil
2 tablespoons butter
4 ducks, halved lengthwise
3 tablespoons flour
2 cups chicken broth
1/2 cup sherry
Salt and pepper to taste

Heat olive oil and butter in a heavy skillet; cook ducks until browned. Place ducks in a 2 1/2-quart casserole. Add flour to pan drippings and lightly brown. Stir in broth and sherry. Season to taste. Pour over ducks, cover and bake at 350°F for 1 hour or until tender.

<u>SERVES 4</u>

Tip: Wild rice complements the duck.

Waterfowl

GRILLED GOOSE BREAST FILLETS

Goose breast fillets
Red wine (such as Merlot or Burgundy)
1 garlic clove, minced
Salt and pepper
Poultry seasoning
Butter

Fillet goose breasts and marinate in red wine and minced garlic. Use enough wine to barely cover breasts. Refrigerate while marinating (4 - 24 hours). Grill breast fillets for 8 - 10 minutes per side, sprinkle with salt, pepper and poultry seasoning, and baste with melted butter while grilling. Slice breasts on diagonal and serve with melted butter.

Tip: These can be grilled in a grilling pan or on a charcoal or gas grill. Use as an appetizer or main course. Do not overcook. Goose should be cooked either rare or medium rare.

HUNTING DAY CREAMY DUCK

8 duck breasts, skinned and cut into small pieces
Salt and pepper
Small amount of cooking oil
1 medium onion, chopped
2 (10¾-ounce) cans cream of mushroom soup
1 (10¾-ounce) can beef consommé
½-1 cup water
1 teaspoon Worcestershire sauce

Sprinkle duck pieces with salt and pepper and lightly brown in a small amount of oil. Place duck on paper towels to drain. Sauté onions in oil after cooking duck. Meanwhile place remaining ingredients in crockpot and stir well. Add water as needed to make a creamy mixture. (Do not add too much water because the steam from the covered crockpot adds more moisture.) Stir in duck pieces and onion. Cover and cook on low for 6 - 8 hours (or high for 2 - 4 hours). Serve over rice, pasta, toast points or biscuits.

Tip: How delightful to have this ready when you return from a day of hunting.

OVEN DUCK OR GOOSE

¼ cup finely chopped onion
2 tablespoons butter or margarine, melted
1 (10¾-ounce) can cream of mushroom soup
4 ounces frozen orange juice concentrate, thawed
1 tablespoon soy sauce
2 tablespoons freshly squeezed lemon juice
½ cup red wine
2 ducks, halved or 1 goose, cut up
Salt and pepper to taste

Sauté onion in butter and add to soup, orange juice, soy sauce, lemon juice and wine. Mix together well. Pat ducks or goose dry with a paper towel and sprinkle with salt and pepper. Place birds in roasting pan and pour soup mixture over all. Cover and bake at 300°F for 3 - 3½ hours or until tender. Serve pan juices over birds.

DUCK APPETIZER STRIPS

Duck breasts, skin removed
Flour
Salt and pepper
1 egg, lightly beaten
¼ cup milk
Butter

Cut duck breasts into strips approximately ½ inch by 3 inches. Season flour with salt and pepper. In separate dish, combine egg and milk. Lightly flour duck strips, dip in milk/egg mixture, and dredge in flour again. Fry in butter until golden brown and crisp. Serve with ranch or honey mustard dressing for a delicious appetizer.

Tip: Try these as an entrée with rice and gravy.

STEVE'S DUCK JERKY

Cut duck into ⅛-inch-thick pieces. For chewier jerky, slice lengthwise along breast.

Marinate duck fillet strips in a mixture that is ½ soy sauce, ¼ Worcestershire sauce, and ¼ liquid smoke. Marinate over night. Arrange on dehydrator and sprinkle with garlic pepper.

Dehydrate until desired dryness is reached.

SOUPS, STEWS & CHILI

Whether the setting is the family kitchen, a remote cabin or a tent camp, there is something special about sitting down to a hearty meal that features piping hot soup, stew or chili. Dishes of this type lend themselves to reheating or to situations where a crockpot can be set to simmering at dawn as the hunter takes to the field, secure in the knowledge that upon his dog-tired return at day's end, sustaining fare awaits him. Another great virtue of dishes of this type is that they are ideally suited to utilizing leftovers,

inferior cuts of meat, or to the creation of what old-timers in the North Carolina mountains used to call slumgullion: You simply take what is available, add some vegetables, stock or chili powder and eureka, a tasty dish is the result.

While the recipes below are ones that work for us, honesty compels us to admit that many are in greater or lesser degree the product of happenstance or chance. Throw in a bit of this or that, always remembering that one or more game meats form the basis upon which you build, season and sample, and before long you have a dish

no king would disdain.

Experimentation is one of the never-ending delights of game cookery, and nowhere does it come into fuller play than with soups, stews, and chili. In that context, we would encourage you to consider the two dozen recipes that follow as a starting point which invites expansion as you test them and plow new ground based on your own personal preferences in terms of seasonings, how hot you like your chili, and the like.

Member Peter Bocha of Racine, Wisconsin, with a trophy British Columbia Stone sheep.

TURKEY AND WILD RICE SOUP

6 tablespoons butter or margarine
1/2 cup chopped onion
1 cup chopped celery
1/2 cup chopped carrots
1/2 cup sliced fresh mushrooms
6 tablespoons flour
Salt and pepper to taste
2 (10¾-ounce each) cans chicken broth
4 cups milk
2 cups cooked wild rice
2 cups cubed, cooked turkey (I like to use half dark
    meat and half white meat)

Melt butter in a large pan. Sauté onions, celery, carrots and mushrooms until tender crisp. Stir in flour, salt and pepper. Add chicken broth and milk. Stir until thickened. Add wild rice and turkey. Adjust seasonings. Simmer until heated through.

Serves 8

Tip: This is a great way to use the dark wild turkey meat and really adds to the flavor of the soup. Since we like to reserve the wild turkey breasts for very special recipes, our preference is to use cooked chicken breasts along with the dark turkey meat. We prefer the true wild rice, which we order from Minnesota, over the typical kinds seen in most grocery stores. The flavor is superb. There is even a broken wild rice which can be used for soups and is less expensive.

HOME STYLE WILD TURKEY NOODLE SOUP

1 quart homemade stock (see tip under Savory
    Spinach Turkey Soup, this page)
1 rib celery, finely chopped
1 large carrot, finely chopped
1/4 cup finely chopped onion
1 cup chopped leftover wild turkey
1/4 pound thin spaghetti noodles, broken
Salt and pepper to taste

Remove fat from broth. Bring to a boil; add vegetables and cook until vegetables are tender (5 - 8 minutes). Add turkey and noodles and cook until pasta is al denté. Stir several times to keep pasta from sticking together. Salt and pepper to taste.

SAVORY SPINACH TURKEY SOUP

2 tablespoons olive oil
1/2 cup chopped onion
2 large garlic cloves, minced
2 cups peeled, chopped fresh tomatoes
    (canned tomatoes can be used if fresh tomatoes
    are not available)
4 cups turkey stock (see tip)
1/2 cup quick cooking barley
1 (16-ounce) can red kidney beans, drained and rinsed
2 cups cooked, finely chopped, wild turkey dark meat
5 ounces washed, chopped fresh spinach
2 tablespoons chopped fresh basil
Salt and black pepper to taste (we prefer lots of pepper)

Place olive oil in a Dutch oven and sauté onion and garlic until tender but not brown. Add garlic after onions have cooked a bit to prevent garlic from getting too brown. Add tomatoes and simmer for 5 - 10 minutes. Add turkey stock and heat to boiling. Add barley and simmer for 10 minutes. Add kidney beans and dark turkey bits. Heat to boiling and add spinach and basil. Adjust seasonings and cook for 2 - 5 minutes until spinach is tender.

Tips: To prepare turkey and stock place legs, thighs and neck of wild turkey in a Dutch oven. Cover with water. Add 1 medium onion (chopped), 2 ribs celery (chopped), 2 carrots (chopped), 2 bay leaves, salt and pepper. Bring to a boil, cover and simmer until turkey is tender. Remove turkey and cool. Chop turkey finely and remove gristle, skin and any fat. The dark meat makes a thick broth. We like to strain it twice to remove vegetables and bits of bone and foam. This stock is delicious for soups and casseroles. Canned broth is very high in sodium and preparing your own is an easy way to control salt intake.

Many turkey hunters save only the white breast meat, but sound ethics dictate using all edible portions of the bird. This tasty method utilizes the dark meat.

Savory Spinach Turkey Soup

Soups, Stews & Chili

Using leftovers

Often there will be some meat left over from a venison roast, stuffed goose, baked turkey or any of countless other game dishes. There are endless ways to make use of such remnants, from cold meat sandwiches to salads or pâtés, but one of the best is to use them in soups or stews.

We make a regular practice of keeping soup containers in the freezer, and any leftovers from game meals go straight into them. When a cold winter day or a prolonged rainy spell seems to cry out for a good pot of soup or a thick stew, all that is necessary to get started is to go to one of these containers in the freezer. It doesn't seem to matter if half a dozen different types of game are in it: When married with some vegetables and a tomato juice base in a big pot, then simmered for a time, the end result is an inviting aroma wafting through the house and calling us to the dinner table.

HERBED WHITE BEAN AND SAUSAGE SOUP

| $1\frac{1}{2}$ tablespoons olive oil |
| 2 cups chopped onion |
| 1 cup chopped carrots |
| 2 teaspoons minced garlic |
| 1 teaspoon dried basil |
| 1 teaspoon dried thyme |
| 1 teaspoon dried oregano |
| 1 whole bay leaf |
| 2 cups chopped and peeled tomatoes |
| 16 ounces dried navy (or other white) beans (see tip) |
| 6 cups chicken stock (or water and stock) |
| 1 ham hock |
| $\frac{1}{2}$ pound browned, crumbled, bulk venison sausage |
| 1 (10-ounce) package frozen spinach, defrosted and drained |
| Salt and pepper to taste |

In large soup pot over medium high heat, heat olive oil and sauté onions, carrots and garlic. Add dried herbs and bay leaf and sauté for 1 minute. Add tomatoes, drained navy beans, chicken stock or water, and ham hock. Bring to a boil. Lower heat and simmer until beans are tender (do not let liquid cook away completely; add more liquid if necessary) for about $1\frac{1}{2}$ hours.

Remove ham hock and chop ham. Return chopped ham and browned and crumbled venison sausage to soup. Add spinach and cook for about 1 minute. Adjust salt and pepper. Serve immediately with hot homemade bread or bruschetta.

Tip: Beans can be soaked for 6 - 8 hours or use the quick-soak method: Cover beans with cold water. Bring to a boil; boil for 2 minutes. Cover, remove from heat and let stand for 1 hour. Drain and continue with recipe.

MEATBALL SOUP

1 1/2 pounds ground venison
1/2 cup fine bread crumbs
1 egg
6 cups beef broth or stock
1 cup sliced carrots
1 cup zucchini, cut into 1-inch chunks
1/2 cup chopped onion
1 cup chopped celery
1/3 cup long-grain rice
1 teaspoon salt
1/8 teaspoon pepper
2 bay leaves
1/4 cup ketchup
2 (14-ounce) cans Italian stewed tomatoes, undrained and chopped
1 (8 ounce) can tomato puree

Combine ground venison, bread crumbs and egg; mix well. Shape into 1-inch balls and place 1/2 inch apart in rectangular baking dish or pan (coated with non-stick spray). Bake for 10-15 minutes at 400°F.

Put remaining ingredients in a 5-quart Dutch oven. Add cooked meatballs. Bring to a boil. Reduce heat; cover and simmer for 1 hour or until vegetables and rice are tender. Top soup with freshly grated cheese when served. Crusty French bread goes nicely with this soup.

Tip: A blender does a good job of making fine bread crumbs.

VEGETABLE AND VENISON SOUP

2 large beef or ham bones
5 1/2 cups water
1 pound venison, cut into chunks
2 (16-ounce) cans diced tomatoes
1 tablespoon salt
1 teaspoon black pepper
1 large onion, chopped
1 tablespoon Worcestershire sauce
5 medium carrots, thinly sliced
6-7 large ribs celery, chopped
5-6 medium potatoes, cubed
1 (20-ounce) package frozen green beans
1 (20-ounce) package frozen corn
1 (10-ounce) package frozen lima beans
1/2 cup barley
1 teaspoon sugar
1/2 medium head cabbage, sliced

In large soup pot, place bones, water, venison, tomatoes, salt, pepper and onion. Bring to a boil, reduce heat and simmer for 2 hours or until meat begins to fall apart. Remove soup bones and add all ingredients except cabbage. Cook until potatoes are tender. Add cabbage and cook until cabbage is tender. Serve with homemade cornbread or crusty French bread for a hearty meal.

YIELDS 6 QUARTS

Tip: This soup makes such a large quantity that you may want to freeze several quarts for a quick heat-up dinner on one of those busy, hectic days.

SQUIRREL AND VENISON STEW

2 squirrels
3-4 chicken pieces (legs or thighs)
1 pound venison, cubed
1 cup sliced celery
1 medium onion, chopped
Salt and pepper to taste
1 (46-ounce) can tomato juice
1 (10-ounce) package frozen corn
1 (10-ounce) package frozen green beans
4 medium potatoes, cubed
3 carrots, chopped
1 (10-ounce) package frozen green peas

Combine squirrel, chicken, venison, celery, onion, salt and pepper. Cover with water. Cook until meat is almost tender. Add tomato juice, corn, green beans, potatoes, carrots and peas. Cook until tender. Remove bones and serve with hot bread.

SERVES 6 - 8

SQUIRREL BRUNSWICK STEW

2 squirrels, cut up
1 1/2 teaspoons salt
1 onion, minced
2 (10-ounce) packages frozen lima beans
2 (10-ounce) packages frozen corn
1/2 pound bacon, finely chopped
4 potatoes, peeled and chopped
1 teaspoon pepper
2 teaspoons sugar
2 (14-ounce) cans diced tomatoes
1/4 pound butter, cut into walnut-size pieces
Flour

Cut squirrels into pieces. Heat 4 quarts water to boiling; add salt, onion, beans, corn, bacon, potatoes, pepper and squirrel pieces. Return to a boil, reduce heat, cover and simmer for 2 hours. Add sugar and tomatoes; simmer for an additional hour or until squirrels and vegetables are tender. Ten minutes before completing stew, add butter pieces rolled in flour. (This helps thicken and flavor stew.) Heat to boiling again and adjust seasonings.

PHEASANT PAPRIKASH

2 tablespoons canola oil
1 large onion, chopped
1 large green pepper, sliced (optional)
Paprika - 1 teaspoon or more (use amount you prefer)
1 large fresh tomato, chopped or 1 (14-ounce) can diced tomatoes
Few dashes red pepper
Few dashes black pepper
2 pheasants, cut up
Salt to taste
2 tablespoons flour
1 cup milk

Place canola oil in Dutch oven and heat. Add onions and sauté until tender. Add green pepper slices and cook for a few minutes. Add enough paprika to make a deep red color and stir constantly for about 1 minute. Add tomato, a few dashes each of red pepper and black pepper. Place pheasant pieces in Dutch oven and add enough water to cover pheasant. Add salt. Bring to a boil, reduce heat, cover and simmer for 2 hours or until pheasant is tender. Mix flour and milk; add to mixture. Adjust seasonings. Let come to a boil but do not boil after adding milk. Serve in bowls over noodles of your choice such as ziti, macaroni or shells.

Tip: Since this is really a cold weather dish, we prefer to use a can of tomatoes instead of the fresh, store-bought tomatoes (which seem to have no flavor in December). Also, when we use canned tomatoes, we add less water and like the richer tomato flavor. Since everyone has to work around the bones, we serve this for a family night dinner with homemade bread and green salad.

SAUERBRATEN

2 pounds venison, cut into chunks
1 (10¾-ounce) can beef broth
1/3 cup packed brown sugar
1/3 cup cider vinegar
1/2 cup finely chopped onion
3/4 cups water
10-12 ginger snaps, crushed

Place all ingredients except ginger snaps in crockpot. Cook on high about 6 hours or until venison is tender. Add crushed ginger snaps and stir until thickened.

CROCKPOT ONION AND GAME STEW

1 pound game chunks (venison, duck, rabbit or
    whatever you prefer)
3-4 medium potatoes, chopped
1 medium onion, chopped
2 carrots, chopped
2 ribs celery, chopped
1 cup sliced fresh mushrooms
1 (10¾-ounce) can onion soup
½ soup can wine
½ soup can water
Black pepper to taste
1 (5-ounce) package frozen green peas

Place meat, potatoes, onion, carrots, celery and
mushrooms in crockpot and barely cover with
onion soup, wine and water. Cook on medium
for about 6 hours or until meat and vegetables
are tender. Add peas and increase heat to high.
Cook until peas are tender. Thicken stew if
desired with a flour and water paste. Serve with
hot sourdough bread.

SIMPLE OVEN STEW

¼ cup flour
½ teaspoon salt
¼ teaspoon pepper
2 pounds venison stew meat, cut into 1-inch pieces
3-4 tablespoons canola oil
4-5 medium potatoes, peeled and cut into chunks
4-5 carrots, cut into chunks
2 ribs celery, cut into chunks
1 package dry onion soup mix
3 cups water

Mix flour, salt and pepper in a paper bag. Add
venison and shake well. Brown meat in canola
oil and place in large casserole. Add potatoes,
carrots, celery, soup and water. Cover and cook
at 325°F for 2 hours or until meat and vegetables are tender.

QUICK ITALIAN SOUP

½ pound ground venison
¼ cup chopped onion
1 (14-ounce) can Italian stewed tomatoes
1 (16-ounce) can peeled tomatoes, chopped
1 (10½-ounce) can double-rich beef broth
1 (8-ounce) can mixed vegetables, drained
½ cup canned kidney beans, drained
1 (5-ounce) package frozen chopped spinach, defrosted
1 teaspoon Italian seasoning
¼ teaspoon garlic salt
1 teaspoon parsley
¼ teaspoon pepper
½ cup uncooked macaroni noodles

In large saucepan or Dutch oven, brown venison
and onion. Add tomatoes, broth, vegetables,
beans and seasonings. Bring to a boil; add noodles. Reduce heat to medium and cook for 10 -
15 minutes or until macaroni noodles are done.

SERVES 4 - 6

VENISON NOODLE SOUP

4 cups beef broth
¼-½ pound egg noodles or spaghetti
½ pound ground venison
2 ribs celery, chopped
1 small onion, chopped
2 tablespoons butter or margarine
Garlic salt to taste
Salt and pepper to taste
Chives and Parmesan cheese

Heat broth to boiling and add noodles. In separate
pan, brown venison. Sauté celery and onion in
butter. When noodles are done, add cooked venison, celery and onion to soup pot. Add garlic salt,
salt and pepper to taste. Simmer for 10 - 15 minutes. Garnish with fresh chives and Parmesan.

Tip: Leftover cooked burgers can be chopped and used
in the soup.

QUICK AND SIMPLE CHILI

1-2 pounds ground or chopped venison
1 large onion, chopped
1 (14-ounce) can tomatoes, diced
1 (16-ounce) can drained and rinsed beans
   (kidney or pinto)
1 (6-ounce) can tomato paste
1 cup water
1 package chili seasoning
Salt and pepper to taste

Brown venison and onion. Add tomatoes, beans, tomato paste, water and seasonings. Simmer for 45 minutes or longer for flavors to blend. Serve hot, topped with grated cheese and chives.

Tip: Substitute taco seasoning for chili seasoning and go Mexican with tacos or burritos. Using the pre-packaged seasoning mixes is easy; however, we like to add our own seasonings (chili powder, garlic, red pepper and/or cumin) instead of using a mix. That makes it easy to add only the flavors we like and to adjust the "heat" accordingly.

NORTHERN CHILI

2 pounds ground or chopped venison

2 tablespoons canola oil

1 cup chopped onion

1 (6-ounce) can tomato paste

1 teaspoon cinnamon

1 teaspoon black pepper

1/2 teaspoon cayenne pepper

1/2 teaspoon ground cumin

1/2 teaspoon ground allspice

2 tablespoons Worcestershire sauce

2 teaspoon salt

1 tablespoon vinegar

1 bay leaf

1 cup red wine

3 cups water, divided

In a large kettle brown venison in canola oil with the onion; add tomato paste, cinnamon, black pepper, cayenne, cumin, allspice, Worcestershire sauce, salt, vinegar, bay leaf, wine and 2 cups of the water. Heat mixture to boiling. Simmer, stirring occasionally, for 1 hour; add remaining 1 cup of the water and simmer, stirring occasionally, for 2 hours more. Discard bay leaf before serving.

<u>Serves 6 - 8</u>

Tip: Some people prefer their chili without beans; this is one to try.

CHILI IN THE CROCKPOT

2 pounds ground (or chopped) venison

1 medium onion, diced

1 cup fresh sliced mushrooms

1 garlic clove, minced

1 bell pepper, chopped (optional)

2 ribs celery, chopped

2 tablespoons canola oil

2 (16-ounce) cans kidney beans, rinsed and drained

2 (16-ounce) cans tomatoes, undrained

1 1/2 tablespoons sugar

1 tablespoon Worcestershire sauce

1 package chili seasonings (or 1 1/2-2 tablespoons chili powder)

1-3 cups water

Salt and pepper to taste

Brown venison, onion, mushrooms, garlic, bell pepper and celery in canola oil. Place in crockpot and add all other ingredients. Mix well; cook on medium for 6 - 8 hours.

THE CHILI CONNECTION

The marvels that chili powder brings to game are virtually boundless. Chili can be a main dish, accompanied by crackers or cornbread and maybe a salad or piece of fruit, but it can also be seen as a condiment.

A hot dog or hamburger drenched in chili to the point where it requires a fork to eat is one way to get a meal ready in a hurry, and even teenagers likely to turn up their noses at more elaborate fare will dig right in. Or try adding zest to your chili with raw onions or green peppers sprinkled over the top. If you are one of those hardy souls with a steel-lined stomach who thinks you aren't eating right until the food is so spicy you can feel the heat coming out of the top of your head, chop up some chili peppers to add zing to the chili powder you have already used. And of course, don't overlook the way melted cheese and chili unite to form a tasty pair.

FEASTS & FLAVORS FROM
NATURE'S GARDEN

Man has always been a hunter and a gatherer, and the preceding chapters have focused on the hunting side of our heritage. Historically speaking though, the process of gathering has loomed much larger in man's livelihood through the ages than has hunting. Accordingly, it seems only fitting that we conclude with a selection of recipes that feature some of the incredibly varied bounty available in nature's garden. Wild vegetables, mushrooms, nuts, fruits and berries are our focus here, and throughout the cookbook a special effort has been made to offer recipes where these foods are used in conjunction with meat. Likewise, they figure prominently in the full menus concluding each chapter.

Gathering wild foods can be great family fun, something of an adventure, and a useful connection with the ways of our forefathers. Moreover, the flavors of the wild often make those of domesticated counterparts seem tame by comparison. No commercially grown strawberries can, for example, match the sweetness and taste of the red jewels found growing in the meadows of spring. Nor can loganberries or garden black-

berries come close to matching the taste of those gathered from the wild, with juice-stained hands and a few briar pricks being the honorable signs of work well done.

Any good hunter realizes that consistent success involves paying his dues in terms of scouting, preseason planning and other aspects of readying one's self for the actual hunt. While the simple process of gathering fruits, nuts, berries and other wild foods offers its own rewards in the form of fine eating and simple self-satisfaction, there are further rewards to be reaped as well. You may well discover, when picking blackberries, that a particular briar thicket is a favorite bedding place for deer, or an afternoon search for morels just might lead you to a roosting site regularly used by turkeys.

Nature produces great bounty beyond game meat.

In truth, any time you venture afield there is something to be learned. When Horace Kephart, the author of *Camping and Woodcraft* (and widely hailed as the Dean of American Campers), commented that "in the school of the outdoors there is no graduation day," he surely knew whereof he spoke. In that context, it might also be worth noting that Kephart was an exceptional game cook, as another of his books, *Camp Cookery*, reveals.

Take the time to wander through the wilds at all seasons, not merely as a hunter but as a gatherer of food and knowledge. You will soon discover that the process will make you a better hunter and an improved woodsman, not to mention that the efforts will bring new and novel tastes to your table.

WILD STRAWBERRY TRIFLE

1 yellow cake mix, baked according to directions

1 quart wild strawberries (cooked slightly with sugar and a dash or two of Grand Marnier or other orange liqueur)—reserve some fresh berries to decorate top

3 large vanilla pudding mixes (enough for 6 cups of milk), mixed according to directions

2 large whipped topping (24 ounces total)

Cover bottom of large bowl (or trifle dish) with a layer of crumbled cake. Place a layer of strawberries over cake, followed by a layer of pudding and a layer of whipped topping. Repeat layers twice, ending with whipped topping and reserved fresh berries.

SERVES 16

Tip: This is a versatile recipe and works well with other berries. Chocoholics should try this with chocolate cake or brownies, chocolate pudding, and crushed toffee pieces.

WILD STRAWBERRY FREEZER JAM

2 cups crushed wild strawberries

4 cups sugar

1 package fruit pectin

³⁄4 cup water

Combine strawberries and sugar, mixing thoroughly; set aside for 10 minutes and stir occasionally. Mix pectin with water in a small saucepan. Bring to a boil and boil for 1 minute, stirring constantly. Remove from heat, add to fruit and stir constantly for 3 minutes. Pour quickly into sterilized glass or plastic containers with tight-fitting lids. Cover immediately. Let containers stand at room temperature for 24 hours. Place jam in the freezer. Frozen jam may be thawed in a microwave oven. Measurements must be exact for jam to set.

Tip: For raspberries, blueberries or blackberries, use 3 cups crushed berries and 5¹⁄4 cups sugar.

WILD STRAWBERRY SPINACH SALAD

4 cups washed and torn spinach
1 cup hulled, rinsed and drained wild strawberries
1 kiwi, peeled and sliced (optional)
2/3 cup chopped macadamia nuts

Combine spinach, strawberries, kiwi and nuts. Set aside.

DRESSING

2 tablespoons strawberry jam
2 tablespoons cider vinegar
1/3 cup oil

Place jam and vinegar in blender and process until blended. Add oil gradually while you continue to process. (This works best if you have a small opening in your blender top to add the oil.) Pour desired amount of dressing over salad and toss gently.

SERVES 4

Tips: If you are fortunate enough to have access to tender dandelion greens, they can be used in place of the spinach.

Try wild raspberries and raspberry jam for a nice change.

Life Member Mark Dotter of White Haven, Pennsylvania, with an Idaho bull elk.

CHESTNUT DRESSING

1/2 cup butter or margarine
1 cup finely chopped celery
1 cup finely chopped onion
1 cup cooked, chopped, chestnuts (see tip)
6-8 cups cornbread crumbs (homemade is better)
1 egg, beaten
2 (or more) cups chicken broth
Salt, pepper and sage to taste

Melt butter in skillet and sauté celery, onion and chestnuts. Cook slowly over low heat for 10 minutes; stir frequently as this burns easily. Add to cornbread crumbs in mixing bowl. Add beaten egg and broth; mix well. Dressing must be VERY moist; add more liquid if necessary. Season to taste with salt, pepper and sage. Bake in casserole dish at 350°F for 30 - 45 minutes or until golden brown.

Tip: To prepare chestnuts, cut an X on the round side of each chestnut with a sharp knife. Place in a saucepan, add water to cover and simmer chestnuts until they are tender (about 45 minutes). Shell and peel while warm. You can buy a nifty little inexpensive gadget for cutting the X in chestnuts that is safer and easier to use than a knife.

CHESTNUT SAUCE

3 tablespoons butter
3 tablespoons flour
1 cup milk
1/2 cup whipping cream
Salt and freshly ground black pepper to taste
Dash of nutmeg
1 cup cooked, finely chopped, chestnuts

Melt butter in saucepan. Add flour and stir constantly to cook flour. Add milk and cream; stir until thickened. Season with salt, pepper and nutmeg. Add chestnuts to sauce and heat through. Serve with venison or game birds.

Berry Crisp

BERRY CRISP

1 cup uncooked oats, quick cooking or regular
   (not instant)

1 cup all-purpose flour

1 cup packed brown sugar

1/4-1/2 cup chopped nuts (walnuts, pecans, or
   hazelnuts)

1/2 cup butter or margarine (cold)

3 cups fresh or frozen berries, such as wild
   strawberries, wild raspberries, wild blackberries,
   huckleberries or gooseberries

1/2 cup sugar (or desired amount)

Mix oats, flour and brown sugar. Add nuts. Cut in butter or margarine until crumbly. Grease or spray an 8-inch square pan. Place half of crumb mixture on bottom. Mix berries and white sugar and pour over crumb mixture. Top with remaining crumb mixture. Bake at 350°F for 30 - 45 minutes or until golden brown and bubbly. Serve warm with ice cream or whipped cream.

STRAWBERRY BUTTER

1 cup salted butter (at room temperature)
2 teaspoons - 3 tablespoons powdered sugar
¾ cup wild strawberries, hulled, rinsed and drained well

Cut butter into pieces and place in a blender. Pulse until light. Add desired amount of sugar and berries; blend until spread is light and fluffy. Refrigerate in a covered container.

Tip: Here is a recipe that will make a few tasty, wild strawberries go a long way. There are numerous uses for this flavored butter: hot flaky biscuits, croissants, rolls, toast, English muffins, bagels, pancakes or waffles, tea or party sandwiches. Strawberry butter can make a Sunday brunch special.

STRAWBERRY MUFFINS

1 cup self-rising flour
¾ cup sugar
1 egg, beaten
¼ cup milk
¼ cup canola oil
½-1 cup wild strawberries

TOPPING

¼ cup sugar
⅛-¼ teaspoon cinnamon

Using a spoon, mix all muffin ingredients except strawberries until thoroughly mixed. Gently fold in strawberries and fill sprayed muffin tins ⅔ full. Combine sugar and cinnamon and sprinkle over top of muffins. Bake at 375°F for 15 - 20 minutes or until lightly browned. Serve warm with strawberry butter or strawberry cream cheese.

SERVES 12

Tips: This is a great way to "stretch" a small amount of fruit.
Wild strawberries are so sweet that the muffins are like dessert. These muffins are much better served immediately from the oven; they do not reheat well. Blueberries may be substituted for the strawberries.

WILD BERRY COBBLER

1 cup all-purpose flour
1 cup sugar
2 teaspoons baking powder
1 cup milk
¼ cup butter, melted
2-4 cups fresh blackberries, dewberries, elderberries, huckleberries, raspberries, or strawberries

Combine flour, sugar, baking powder and milk; stir with a wire whisk until smooth. Add melted butter and blend. Pour batter into 9 x 13-inch baking dish. Pour berries (amount depends on personal preference) evenly over batter. Do not stir. Bake at 350°F for 30 - 40 minutes or until golden brown. Serve warm with vanilla ice cream, whipped topping or milk.

SERVES 6 - 8

Tip: Leftovers may be reheated in a microwave oven. Sweeten berries if needed.

DANDELION GREENS

4 cups dandelion greens
1 small onion, chopped
1 garlic clove, minced
½ cup finely diced ham
2 tablespoons olive oil
2 teaspoons lemon juice
Salt and pepper to taste

Boil greens 2 minutes and drain well. Sauté onion, garlic and ham in olive oil until onion is tender. Add boiled greens along with lemon juice, salt and pepper. Serve immediately.

ELAINE'S BLUEBERRY COBBLER

1/2 stick butter or margarine

4 cups fresh blueberries, rinsed and drained
   (frozen berries may be used, but drain well)

1 teaspoon freshly squeezed lemon juice

3/4-1 cup sugar

TOPPING

1 cup self-rising flour

1 cup sugar

1 teaspoon vanilla flavoring

1/2 cup milk

Preheat oven to 375°F. Melt butter in 8 x 8-inch baking dish in the microwave. Combine blueberries and lemon juice in bowl; add sugar and mix well. Spoon blueberries into baking dish over melted butter; do not stir. Combine flour and sugar in small bowl. Add vanilla to milk and mix into flour and sugar. Pour topping over blueberries and bake for 30 - 45 minutes or until bubbly and golden brown. Serve with whipped cream or vanilla ice cream.

Tip: Try this recipe with blackberries, dewberries or raspberries.

FRESH BLUEBERRY PIE

1 baked 9-inch pie shell (pastry or graham cracker)

4 cups fresh blueberries, divided

1 cup sugar

3 tablespoons cornstarch

1/4 cup water

1/4 teaspoon salt

1/4 teaspoon cinnamon

1 tablespoon butter

Line pie shell with 2 cups of the fresh blueberries. Cook remaining 2 cups of the berries with sugar, cornstarch, water and salt over medium heat until thickened. Remove from heat. Add cinnamon and butter and cool slightly. Pour over berries in shell. Refrigerate. Serve with whipped topping.

EASY BLUEBERRY BUCKLE

4 cups fresh blueberries

1/2 cup maple syrup

1 teaspoon cinnamon

1/4 cup cornstarch

1 1/4 cups flour

3/4 cup brown sugar

1/2 cup butter, softened

1/2 teaspoon almond extract

Gently stir blueberries, maple syrup, cinnamon and cornstarch. Pour into 9-inch square baking dish that has been sprayed. In separate bowl, blend flour and brown sugar. Cut butter and almond extract into flour and sugar until mixture is crumbly. Sprinkle over berries and bake at 375°F for 30 - 45 minutes or until lightly browned and bubbly. Serve warm with ice cream, whipped cream or milk.

SERVES 6

BLUEBERRY SALAD

2 cups frozen or fresh blueberries

1 (6-ounce) package black cherry gelatin

1 cup water

1 (8 1/2-ounce) can crushed pineapple, undrained

1 small carton whipped topping

1 (3-ounce) package cream cheese, softened

1/2 cup finely chopped nuts

Drain blueberries, reserving juice. Add enough water to blueberry juice to make 2 cups. Heat juice to boiling and add gelatin; stir until gelatin is dissolved. Add 1 cup cold water, pineapple and blueberries. Pour into 9 x 13-inch dish and refrigerate until firm.

Beat softened cream cheese, add nuts and fold in whipped topping. Mix well. Spread over congealed salad and chill for at least 2 hours before serving.

Tip: If you use fresh blueberries, place one cup of berries in a saucepan, cover with water and simmer until berries are tender. Drain and continue as directed above but add both the cooked and fresh berries. The contrast in raw and cooked berries is appealing. Huckleberries may be easily substituted in this recipe.

BLACKBERRY DUMPLINGS

1 quart blackberries

1 cup sugar (or to taste)

Enough water to make berries thin enough to
*   cook dumplings*

DUMPLINGS

1 cup flour

2 teaspoons baking powder

1/4 teaspoon salt

1 tablespoon sugar

1 cup milk

Place blackberries, sugar and water in saucepan and heat to boiling. Meanwhile, mix dumpling ingredients thoroughly and drop by tablespoons into boiling berries. Cook for 15 minutes or until dumplings are cooked through the center. Serve hot with cream.

COLD BLACKBERRY SOUP

4 cups rinsed blackberries

1 banana

1 cup sweet pineapple juice

1 cup sour cream

1 tablespoon raspberry liqueur

Place all ingredients in food processor and pulse until blended. Chill. Serve in soup bowls, champagne glasses or tea cups. Serve with toasted pound cake.

Tip: To toast pound cake, cut cake slices with a cookie cutter and place under the broiler until cake is lightly browned. Dip edges of cake in melted chocolate and serve with chilled blackberry soup.

BLACKBERRY SORBET

2 1/2 cups boiling water

1 tea bag (regular size)

3 cups fresh blackberries

1 1/4 cups sugar

1/4 cup freshly squeezed lemon juice (about 1 1/2 lemons)

Pour boiling water over tea bag and steep for 10 minutes. Mix blackberries with sugar. Add tea to the berries; crush berries with the back of a spoon to release juices. Cover and cool. Purée berry/tea mixture in food processor using a metal blade. Divide mixture if necessary. Strain through a fine sieve. Add lemon juice and mix. Refrigerate for at least 1 hour. Place sorbet mixture in ice cream maker and process according to manufacturers' instructions. Freeze sorbet overnight to allow flavors to develop. Makes 1 quart.

WILD BLACKBERRY SAUCE

2 cups blackberries

1/2-3/4 cup sugar

1 tablespoon fresh lemon juice

Mix all ingredients well and refrigerate for 1 hour or more. Allow sauce to come to room temperature before serving. Delicious served over a chocolate tart, cheesecake or ice cream.

WILD RASPBERRY SAUCE

2 cups fresh or frozen wild raspberries

4 tablespoons sugar

1-2 tablespoons Grand Marnier liqueur

Place berries, sugar and liqueur in a small saucepan. Bring to a boil and reduce heat. Simmer for 2 - 3 minutes or until berries are tender. Press through a sieve to remove seeds. Serve over ice cream, cheesecake, pound cake, waffles, French toast or pancakes.

RASPBERRY VINEGAR

1/2-1 cup raspberries

1 cup white vinegar

Wash berries and drain well. Place fruit in a pretty bottle. Heat vinegar and pour over fruit. Let cool before putting the top on the bottle. Corks are good to use for a top. Keep in a cool place for 7 days before tasting. If you taste the flavor of the fruit, the vinegar is ready. (Set aside for a few more days if you cannot taste the fruit.) You can leave the fruit in the vinegar or strain it out. Store in a cool place.

Tip: Other berries, such as blackberries, blueberries or strawberries, can be used. Flavored vinegars make homemade salad dressings special and are lovely gifts when placed in a special bottle.

HUCKLEBERRY NUT BREAD

3/4 cup sugar

1/2 teaspoon salt

1/4 cup butter or margarine, melted

1 egg

2 cups flour

2 teaspoons baking powder

1/2 teaspoon cinnamon

1/2 cup milk

1 cup huckleberries (if frozen, thaw and drain well)

1/2 cup chopped nuts

Cinnamon sugar to taste

Cream sugar, salt and melted butter. Add egg and beat well. In separate bowl, sift flour, baking powder and cinnamon. Add flour mixture to creamed mixture alternately with milk; blend well. Gently fold huckleberries and nuts into batter. Pour into 9 x 5 x 3-inch prepared loaf pan. Sprinkle a very light coating of cinnamon sugar over bread. Bake at 375°F for 45 minutes or until golden brown and bread tests done in center with a toothpick. Cool in pan for 10 minutes before removing.

HUCKLEBERRY PIE WITH HAZELNUT GLAZE

3 cups fresh (or frozen) huckleberries

1 cup grated apple

1 cup sugar

3 tablespoons flour

1/2 teaspoon almond extract

Several dashes of salt, optional

Pastry for double pie crust

2 tablespoons butter

Mix huckleberries, apple, sugar, flour, almond extract and salt. Pour into unbaked pie shell. Dot with butter. Cover with top crust and bake at 375°F for about 1 hour or until nicely browned. Top with hazelnut glaze when you remove pie from oven.

HAZELNUT GLAZE

1/3 cup packed brown sugar

3 tablespoons light cream

1/2 cup finely chopped toasted hazelnuts

Place brown sugar and cream in small saucepan over low heat and stir constantly until sugar melts. Stir in hazelnuts. Drizzle over hot pie.

Tip: Try this glaze with blackberry or blueberry pie.

ROSEHIP SYRUP

Place cleaned rosehips in measuring cup. Add an equal amount of sugar and half the amount of water. Cook slowly until rosehips mash easily. Mash with potato masher and press through a sieve. Store in refrigerator and serve over pancakes, waffles, French toast or biscuits.

Tip: Here is another way to get your vitamin C.

Cranberry Sauce with Grand Marnier

CRANBERRY SAUCE WITH GRAND MARNIER

1 cup sugar

1 cup water

3 cups fresh whole cranberries

1-2 tablespoons Grand Marnier or orange-flavored liqueur

Combine sugar and water in medium saucepan. Cook over medium heat, stirring constantly, until sugar has dissolved and mixture comes to a boil. Add cranberries and return to a boil. Reduce heat and simmer for about 10 minutes. Stir occasionally. Remove from heat and stir in desired amount of liqueur. Chill until serving time.

Tip: Serve with wild turkey and other wild game.

INDEX